A GUIDE TO
FALLING DOWN
IN PUBLIC

ISBN: 978-1-62124-021-1
Library of Congress Control Number: 2016935642

Published by Breakaway Books
P.O. Box 24
Halcottsville, NY 12438
www.breakawaybooks.com

FIRST EDITION

A GUIDE TO FALLING DOWN IN PUBLIC

Finding Balance On and Off the Bicycle

JOE "METAL COWBOY" KURMASKIE

BREAKAWAY BOOKS
HALCOTTSVILLE, NEW YORK
2016

To Team Zippy!

Stray well + ride on! Cheers,

Joe

CONTENTS

For
Bertha "a little recognition" Kemp,
James "again, with feeling" Wicker,
Jim "staying until we get that sound"
Crosby, and Mary Jane "Fweetbaby" Trout

Beloved teachers of my youth.
Their influence on my writing is surpassed only
by their impact on my character.

DAVID

How prayer works: You pray for the hungry, then you feed them.
—Anonymous

My five-year-old, Sawyer, abandons his breakfast to look out the window. David, our neighborhood Fisher King, is pushing his home on wheels, a roughed-up mountain bike with three trailers snaking behind it. Everything he owns is stacked tall and wide. Sawyer calls it his Grinch-who-stole-Christmas sleigh.

Sometimes David gives Sawyer and Sawyer's older brother, Matteo, toys and refurbished treasures he's rescued. He'll drop off bike wheels that I don't need, which I graciously accept, store, use for school art projects, or just pay forward.

There's a hidden spot by the garage where we put out cans and bottles, sometimes a blanket. We chat every week or so, pedaling side by side for a few blocks, but it's acquaintances at best.

His load, which contracts and expands periodically, never drops below three hundred pounds. Having pulled five hundred pounds of kids and gear across the continent by bicycle, twice, I'm a deadeye at guesstimating rolling loads. Sometimes he weaves and wavers before getting his trailer train up to speed, but I've never seen him fall.

He doesn't let many people near. Perhaps he recognizes something in me and the heavy wheeled loads of human cargo I'm always carrying to the school drop-off, the park, the grocery store. Perhaps it's just that he can't avoid me.

There was that time he split a four-pack of pudding cups with the boys and me last summer. We sat on the rock wall beside the funeral home and ate his chocolate puddings in comfortable silence.

I hear him in heated discussions sometimes, replaying board meetings by the sounds of it, and storming out beyond the Japanese maples with hands thrown up. His conversation falls off to a few mumbles and whispers, then he grabs his bar grips and pushes or pedals the bike train to points nearby, but unknown.

"David must have lost his shoes," Sawyer says. I look out the window. It's forty-five degrees, he's shoeless, trying to mount a bike that today carries north of six hundred pounds.

His legs are a horror. They looked a little rough last summer, but now this . . . angry, scarlet-colored, splotchy, and swollen to the size of spiral hams all the way up his calves.

I guess I was hoping for magic, or someone else to step up. Sawyer turns to me and frowns. I'm rocked by shame. When your five-year-old is a better caretaker of the neighborhood's homeless population, you're failing every which way.

I post a notice on our neighborhood listserve. It can be a bit Nosy Nancy sometimes—and enough already with the complaining about coyote sightings and how we need to lock up our house cats—but it's useful on occasion, and troll-free for the most part.

Neighbors rally with kind words, and one of them, a doctor, says he's also noticed David walking barefoot, and now that he's been called out by a five-year-old, he feels like a proper piece of shit. It's the push he needed. He tells me what to look for and asks if I'll report my findings.

When I see David, I find out that we wear the same shoe size and, maybe it's because I have a hand placed gently on his shoulder and the other on his handlebars, David sticks around for a frank conversation about his current condition. While we chat, he takes to the curb and tries on the shoes.

A perfect fit.

He says he knows he needs a doctor, but keeps putting it off. Mentions something about getting his fishing poles in working order first. I steer the conversation back to his feet. He gets a little worked up talking about how there's the issue of his home on wheels and security if he's going to take a day of bus rides to the mobile clinic (feet, shower, getting back on his meds). If he didn't have to worry about people taking his stuff, well then. He says something about getting a new post office box, too. They won't send his disability checks without one.

The neighborhood doctor, on my findings, made an attempt at contact. David pedaled away when he tried to get close, but Doc could see the extent of the swelling even from a distance.

"It's bad . . . could turn life threatening at any time. He needs medication and . . ." Doc offers a hopeless little laugh. "He needs to get off his feet for a few weeks. No lifting or putting strain on his legs."

Like that's gonna happen.

It's the day I'd coordinated with David to lock his world to my back carport. At 8 a.m. he's a no-show.

Damn. I've given up hope and gone back to writing in the front room when the familiar squeak of my side gate pulls me from my work. David's laboring his bike and an exceptionally heavy load of the neighborhood's discards (he's a wizard at diagnosing, refurbishing, and repurposing what others deem junk) through to my carport! That evening someone knocks on the door. Sawyer throws it open without checking. David wants to tell us that his bike is all there and nothing is missing. He thanks us more than he should. When I asked him how it went he launches into his adventures, opening up like never before.

Foot treatment, social service paperwork, and he looks chipper and showered. Rather than slipping into the evening, David points to the microscope that we have out.

I ask him to come in, but he's reluctant. From the doorway, he points at the box and mentions that he had the same one as a kid. Beth asks him how he thinks the lightbulb could be replaced because we can't get it working. He explains that the process involves turning the compartment it's cradled within, not replacing the lightbulb per se. He talks like an engineer.

With his help we get it working in about fifteen seconds. A number of things get back on some sort of track that day. David stores his bike in my carport a couple of times a month now. The community has been posting less about coyotes and has turned my garage into an informal goods and services drop point for David. The outpouring has spilled over helping other folks in need throughout the area.

Our walls have always displayed a mix of works by name artists collected from around the world who must vie for space with the boys' artwork—batiks, pastels, drawings, and sayings the family has come up with on our own.

A sponge-brushed bear under a blue moon and purple grass hangs over Sawyer's top bunk. Below it reads, BE GOOD TO EACH OTHER, FOR AS LONG AS YOU CAN, WITH WHATEVER YOU'VE GOT, a Sawyer original. He taps it most mornings, and always before bedding down for the the night.

That evening, after songs and my traditional Good night my princes of the Pacific, my kings of the coast, I turn out the lights and tap the sign for the first time.

A benediction for those who have fallen, taken a knee . . . and an invitation to find the strength to stand, saddle up, and pedal on.

Chapter 1

A GUIDE TO FALLING DOWN IN PUBLIC

Sometimes it takes a good fall to let you know where you stand.
—Hayley Williams

They say the trick is learning how to take a punch . . .

But how often does that happen? Better to master the art of falling down, for those times when you can't achieve the perfect dismount.

Velocity, gravity, momentum, all those miles and mistakes, gravel, questionable choices, black ice, "Ah fuck it" decisions, blind spots, pedaling back into the breach before you were ready, that girl who smelled of soap and jasmine and felt like your future, overcooking the curve just when you thought you'd found the inside of the road.

So many ways to go down hard.

When you think about it, life is stunt work done for scale with most of it left on the cutting room floor. If you're still here it means you're needed on the set, so find the strength to scrape yourself off the ground and take some of the dailies with you; songs, scars, friends, memories. The movie ends the same for everyone, but during a few glorious moments there . . .

Naturally, I've done the bulk of my stunt work on a bicycle.

Falling is something of a shock, but not getting back on your chosen rig . . . that's hard to watch. It's about muscle memory. Some do it with style, grace, and dignity, but don't let anyone tell you different, it's about just getting the fuck back up.

Even though the bicycle was my home throughout childhood, for a brief period of time I confused a couch on wheels, a dashboard, and a gas pedal as some sort of salvation, deemed the bike a toy, and shanked my whole existence into the thick rough.

The end of the road for living someone else's life, or at least a pale version of my own, arrived, literally, on a long dark road in the Everglades. It also ended my brief love affair with the American Dream machine, Madison Avenue–fueled Motor City madness.

A soup-thick fog, a corrupt middle manager bilking the state of Florida on the backs of troubled youth, and a wet hot mess of a comedic genius, Bill Hicks, helped me step out from behind the wheel and reclaim my rightful place in the saddle . . . so I could continue a life behind (handle) bars.

I felt at home working and living day in and out with high-risk youth on the edge of the Glades. These were bad boys acting out, not mad men on villainous rampages. They showed their cards: poverty, broken homes, economic and class warfare. It was like playing Go Fish with X-ray vision.

Management was a different story. The hair on the back of my neck stood tall the night I was asked/ordered to drive an especially corrupt team leader to a regional airport sixty miles to the west. Of course it had to be the power-tripping psychopath who wore a gun on his hip several decades before Florida passed open-carry laws.

I'd be using my car and my gas, motivated by vague, sweeping statements by the psychopath regarding promotions and fringe benefits in the future, but really, I was so lost in the rough of my own making that by then I just did what I was told and tried to keep moving.

"Shit, what is this rice rocket? I thought you had a Mustang." He tossed his bag in the back. I heard the handguns clatter against the floorboard. Maybe one change of clothes, the rest, handguns. He paraded one around the ranch on his hip even though it was against regulations and ridiculously dangerous. A camp full of unstable teens with lengthy juvenile rap sheets getting a last chance to fly right, and this former cop or prison guard, washed out of both careers for incompetence at best, thought it wise to flaunt a sidearm. He made everyone call him Rojas even though it was a nickname he had to give himself. Ten minutes in his company made me question, well, everything.

I started the engine. Rojas was wearing a little cocaine on the outside of his nostrils and we were on our way to an airport with a bag of guns in the backseat. Most likely I was now an accessory to multiple felonies. He didn't seem worried about getting the guns beyond security.

"The Mustang's my dad's. This is a—"

Slamming the passenger door cut me off. Rojas's voice cut me off again.

"I don't fucking care! is what this car is. Too bad my flight's tonight, there's a great little whorehouse off Route 21. I'd show you some real Mustangs."

Twenty miles from Fort Myers the fog closed in so tight I slowed to a crawl and prepared to ease off the road. Rojas cackled, "You pull this Japmobile over and see if I don't shoot your ass."

I waited for him to tell me he was just kidding. Instead, he head-banged and beat out a drum solo on the glove box to a Bryan Adams mixtape he'd forced on me. I tried to see five feet beyond the glass. This was no way to live.

I pulled over.

Rojas slammed the door and stomped about in his cowboy boots, pacing in front of the headlights. Mad, coked up, late. I thought he might actually shoot me.

"I might actually shoot you."

He pulled the gun, slow and dramatic, pointed it into the mist, and let three or four rounds fly. This seemed to help a little.

It certainly confirmed that significant changes needed to take place in my life.

He stood in repose. Long enough for me to appreciate the faint glow of swamp gas just beyond the sides of the road. It was nothing like those Scooby-Doo episodes had led me to believe. Frogs could be heard singing electric beyond the glowing curtain of fog.

My pulse slowed; the world hummed and throbbed around and within me. I settled on a simple fact.

One Neanderthal waving his thunderstick does not negate the beauty of the world . . . so that was something, but was it enough?

I chewed hard on the idea of sideswiping him with the tail end of the car. Enough to put him in the swamp while I floored the vehicle into the mist, but if I missed and left him standing, he might get off a lucky shot.

Rojas holstered his sidearm and discovered something underfoot that made him smile. He commenced to repeatedly, and with extreme malice, squash it.

"Fuckin' frogs," he announced coming around to my side of the car. "Move over, I'll drive." All smiles now.

I told him to get back in his seat. If I was going to die on a lonely strip of blacktop in the Everglades it would not be clutching the passenger-side "Oh, Jesus!" Bar while a coked-up piece of work from an Elmore Leonard novel flipped the vehicle I was still making payments on into a swampy culvert.

"Grew some balls, did you?" He laughed his madman laugh back to his seat. I put in Zeppelin and eased back onto the road.

We inched our way through the soup; Rojas vocalizing epitaphs at me and snorting like a bull through the open window.

He hopped out at Departures without as much as a thank-you. Then pounced back through the fog long enough to bang his bag of guns on the hood of my car, cackle, offer a final snort, then ghost into the fog again.

It would be five years before I'd learn how and why Rojas stopped wearing a gun. A few short months after our nightmare run, Rojas was held at gunpoint, with his own gun of course, by one of the troubled youths who'd decided a ride to Miami was in order, or he'd had enough of Rojas's cock-of-the-walk routine with that sidearm.

He was found naked, gagged, bungee-corded inside a port-a-potty along a swankier part of South Miami Beach, his sidearm wedged between his legs, but alive. Inexplicably, he still had a job to return to.

I'm told Rojas stopped wearing guns after that. His cowboy boots remained. No word on how the Everglades frog population fared.

My head ached and my nerves were jangled. I had to buy a room and hunker down for the night. Since I was still on the clock, I called the office; we worked in twenty-four- to forty-eight-hour shifts on weekends. I'd be docked pay and No! they wouldn't cover the hotel room. I could hear someone in the background calling me a pussy, then a whole room of assholes laughing. I almost caved but this wasn't high school. Even though I needed the money, I'd rather be alive to not spend it. Too pissed to sit in my room, I forked over the two-rink minimum and slipped into a back booth of the hotel's comedy club. My plan: Get lit and feel sorry for myself.

Instead, the comic renderings of Bill Hicks blew my mind and lifted my spirits over the next few hours. Hicks was the original honey badger, laying it down, dropping hammers, and savoring the carnage. He could have done thirty minutes and walked, but he made an evening of it, enjoying the give-and-take of outrage and abuse.

A prizefight . . . and he was a ringer.

People listened at first, curious, some awkward laughter, then came the boos, general complaints. Mostly, "Can't you be more like Robin Williams?" He ended his next bit with, "Nanoo, nanoo, you fuckturds." If someone from the audience made the miscalculation of speaking, he would eat them alive on general principle. People outside the blast zone enjoyed that part the best, until he'd turn on them. Incoherent shouting ensued. He'd make fun of that, too.

One woman started crying just because. He hadn't even said anything to her. Some offered fake laughter as a counterpoint, or had they actually found the thread and rhythm of Bill's insanely clever high-wire act? The room filled with the smell of burnt ozone and the fear-sweat stench of a street riot.

People walked; a few threatened him. The walkers returned since where the hell were they gonna go in this fog? He drew the most energy from that. I was choking on laughter and clapping and absolutely beside myself throughout.

A guy at a big table of folks to my left spittle-screamed, "I should go get a tire iron and beat you with it." Bill screamed back, huge smile on his face, "Go ahead. If it's a Florida tire iron then it's probably shaped like a flaccid penis, am I right? Limp and useless, like your dick. Just try hurting me with either of them, you moron. It'll be like beating me with a Gumby toy."

Then he'd pretend to apologize for the patron's unpleasantness, and slip right back into his act as if nothing had happened.

It was a comic bloodbath.

Genuinely funny, offering a take-it-or-leave-it, world-weary, bemused anger while speaking the truth. He tore off people's scabs, and while they were recoiling—stunned and hurt—he'd hunt around for some salt or lemon juice or anything full of acidic wit to pour into the exposed flesh.

Forced at gunpoint to drive through soup-thick fog to the sound of Bryan Adams's greatest hits, this was just what I needed. Then he placed me in his sites, focusing on my platinum-blond hair.

"I shouldn't bite the hand of the only son of a bitch here, besides me, who seems to be enjoying himself, but Jesus, kid, is that your real hair? It's gotta be, right? Guys don't voluntarily ask for the Marilyn Monroe look. Has the president tried to fuck you yet? Seriously, though, does it come with a dimmer switch? It's like an extra spotlight up here. I could fall off the stage I'm not careful. Hurt myself in a hair-related accident."

Someone clapped at that. Hicks looked over.

"Yeah? That make you happy? Physical suffering of others? 'Merica. Can I get a woot, woot?"

Back to me.

"Hey, I'm just fucking with ya, and not because you're built like something Hulk Hogan shat out . . . it's that I might need your head of hair after the show to guide my sleigh out of this shithole." Brilliant. A little bully by the side of the road comes close to shooting me that evening, and I got blown away by a comic genius working way below his weight class in the orange room of the Fort Myers Holiday Inn.

Something clicked for me. Licking the last bit of salt off the rim of my glass and listening to Hicks tell the people who hadn't tuned him out, or walked, how to spot the saddest souls among us.

"You'll find them shuffling the aisles of Costco just loading up on shit they don't need, a look of purchase-panic in their eyes, near closing time, pushing all of it off the shelves with no joy, no reason, no hope."

"More holes in your heart, more crap in your cart!"

It dawned on me that you could be funny, furious, a little sad, *and* tell the truth . . . for a living? The revolution inside me could be felt on a molecular level. It meant I didn't have to lie down and live anxious anymore, chase things everyone else told me I should believe in. And even if I was doing something I believed in with all my heart, if I was doing it with the wrong people, well then, fuck that noise!

Bill Hicks hung the mike on the stand, turned to leave, but came back to it one more time. He leaned in . . . looking right at me.

"Guess what I'm saying is . . . travel light." I didn't quit the ranch the next day, but where it mattered, between my ears, I was already gone. The car went back to the dealer; it would be nine years before I owned another. I bought a bicycle from an old wrench who had a little shop in Lake Placid, Florida. Ponytail turning gray, he'd pedaled a big chunk of the world, coming to a stop so he could make his stand at the edge of the Glades.

For a week I window-shopped while we got to know each other. I'd browse, then we'd sit on the wooden porch drinking RC Colas. Sometimes he'd roll out stories about his wheeled adventures and sometimes we'd just sit. It didn't take much convincing that I could indeed commute twenty-five miles each way to my job at the Last Chance Ranch. In fact, it would be good training for the road ahead. Any gators sunning on the sides of the road would just help my focus and up my pace. Somewhere between sodas and stories, I put in motion a plan to ride a bicycle from Maine to Florida. Who wouldn't want to have stories of their own worth sharing on a porch one day?

For the first time in quite a while, I got the hell back up.

He sold me a Raleigh Alyeska with a full set of Rhode Gear panniers. I loaded it down with stuff I thought I needed for the fifty-mile round trip: tools, water, a few snacks. And when that got too easy I added extra ballast, anything I could find along the way: rocks, branches. I even hauled a damp bag of dirt for one ride.

From there I graduated to trash and recycling: old tires, beer bottles, coolers discarded along the way. There was no sign to indicate it, but one look at my rig it was clear I'd adopted that stretch of highway for beautification.

I only questioned my decision once.

An old tire half submerged in a roadside swamp caught my eye. I strapped it to the back rack without giving it a proper inspection. A few miles later a water moccasin emerged from the tire, disoriented, not particularly menacing, but that could change in a hurry. Without breaking cadence, I managed to reach around, slow and steady, and eject both tire and stowaway with the pop of the bungee. It was a good test of my helmet mirror. If reptiles could form facial expressions, this one had *WTF?* written all it. Without having to turn my head I watched the bewildered snake perform a midair retreat into the tire as it bounced once, twice, four times, before disappearing into a clump of palmetto bushes. That's when I learned dangling bungee cords and moving bicycle wheels don't mix. Some road rash but no broken bones, it was a lesson I didn't have to learn twice.

For show, I'd sprint down the narrow frontage road by the airstrip entrance to my job—where we had the troubled teens digging up stumps or clearing brush. The kids took to offering their roughneck version of cheering each time I pedaled through the gates. Hats waving, flashing of gang symbols, swearing, hoots, a few good-natured flippings of the bird; one of them threw his Nikes at me, high praise.

Even Rojas, after some inane remarks and lewd bike-related nicknames that failed to stick, stopped talking smack and gave me wider berth. A John Wayne poser with a holster is one thing, but a hulking guy emerging day after day from the heated horizon of an Everglades highway, bike loaded to the brim with redneck treasures and recyclables, makes everything else look like dress-up.

As I pedaled past a few of the ranch's involuntary guests, leaning over shovels, Cool Hand Luke–style, turned it into an episode of *At the Movies*, the juvenile delinquent critics edition.

"He be all Highlander and shit."

I gave them a silent nod.

"Please . . . that's a Mad Max muthafucka, right there."

"Truth."

Until I pedaled away for good a few weeks later, staff and kids alike started referring to me as Mad Max. Though it was far from any truth of me, I liked it and made no attempt to correct them.

Bill Hicks was one of those people who burned twice as bright, but only half as long. He died of pancreatic cancer at the age of thirty-two, clutching his dog-eared copy of the *The Hobbit*.

Talk about traveling light.

But not before the world caught up with his incendiary genius. After the Holiday Inn orange room, it didn't take long before he went nova, playing all the late-night talk shows, Vegas, headlining one of HBO's first comedy specials. Following Bill's death, David Letterman did the unprecedented by inviting Bill's mom onto the show, where he apologized to her and the viewers for censoring one of Bill's performances. Then Letterman showed the clip in its entirety.

Even death couldn't keep Bill Hicks from getting back up.

Letterman hugged Bill's mother, pronounced the comic lightning in a bottle, the likes of which we'd not see again, and said that by pulling Hicks's bit the first time, it spoke to flaws in Letterman's own character, not Bill's.

I was in the wind by then, traveling lighter and farther with each adventure, well beyond the pull of TV talk shows, newspapers, society, anything but the sounds of my own exertions, the next traveling companion and the next story just up the road. Thanks to Bill, I was out there, enjoying the ride.

"The world is like a ride in an amusement park, and when you choose to go on it you think it's real because that's how powerful our minds are. The ride goes up and down, around and around, it has thrills and chills, and it's very brightly colored, and it's very loud, and it's fun for a while. Many people have been on the ride a long time, and they begin to wonder, "Hey, is this real, or is this just a ride?" And other people have remembered, and they come back to us and say, "Hey, don't worry; don't be afraid, ever, because this is just a ride." And we . . . kill those people. "Shut him up! I've got a lot invested in this ride, shut him up! Look at my furrows of worry, look at my big bank account, and my family. This has to be real." It's just a ride. But we always kill the good guys who try and tell us that, you ever notice that? And let the demons run amok . . . But it doesn't matter, because it's just a ride. And we can change it any time we want. It's only a choice. No effort, no work, no job, no savings of money. Just a simple choice, right now, between fear and love. The eyes of fear want you to put bigger locks on your doors, buy guns, close yourself off. The eyes of love instead see all of us as one. Here's what we can do to change the world, right now, to a better ride. Take all that money we spend on weapons and defenses each year and instead spend it feeding and clothing and educating the poor of the world, which it would pay for many times over, not one human being excluded, and we could explore space, together, both inner and outer, forever, in peace." —Bill Hicks

Chapter 2

HOW TO OUTSPRINT AN ELEPHANT

Somewhere in Africa the elephants have a secret grave where they go to lie down, unburden their wrinkled gray bodies, and soar away, light spirits at the end.

—Robert McCammon, *Boy's Life*

The elephants seemed more bemused than riled up by our presence on their trails. The giraffes simply turned their necks in slow motion to take a second look. The warthogs, though, they scared like quail flushed from hiding, and every time three or four darted among the bikes in our pack, the guide reminded us that if one rider went down, the rest of us had to push on—bush rules.

Logical. Maybe necessary. But still a little more harsh than one might have reasonably expected of a charity ride.

It was a little past first light on the first day of the Tour de Tuli Mapungubwe Route, a weeklong affair through South Africa, Botswana, and Zimbabwe that raises money to send the region's children to environmental education programs.

For 12,900 rand (about $1,840), riders get a private tent, all meals plus morning and afternoon snacks (during breaks that, hewing to the remnant traditions of British colonization, were called "tea"), logistical and mechanical support, and expert—if sometimes Darwinian—guides.

More than three hundred of us were there in 2009, split into groups of twenty or so. The most aggressive packs, like mine, had to cover up to 120 kilometers of trail a day on everything from singletrack to long stretches of deep sand to somewhat dry riverbeds. More casual riders could take slightly "easier," shorter routes (about eighty kilometers on average).

The night before, as part of our send-off, Botswana's minister of tourism had told us all a fable involving a rat, a snake, a cow, and an old farming couple. The story was an allegory meant to remind us of the connectedness of everything—cyclists, wild game, even Robert Mugabe, the erratic Zimbabwean dictator whose country our trip would enter and exit several times.

Officially, we had permission to cross the border. In reality, official decrees don't carry much weight here—and the worst that might happen was beyond anyone's guess.

Bush rules. Anyway, I was just hoping for enough connectivity to keep me attached to my group. The crew of stiff-lipped hammerheads I'd been assigned to was led by a man captaining a full-suspension tandem mountain bike in a way that let you know he was muscling over the sand not despite his stoker wife but because with her on the back he could enjoy some extra burden.

His fixed gaze was a blink or two shy of madness, and he drove us onward until we overtook all but the pack made of retired racers from Europe and South Africa's national cricket champion, who smiled easy but rode harder than anything else moving through the thick sand.

We managed to lose sight of him and the pros on a descent. We accomplished this by keeping our heads down and our cranks blurring all the way past the course marker—a pile of weathered rocks with a faint chalk arrow drawn below it.

"Take a few ticks off the clock, then we're back at it," our leader said by way of announcing a break once we were back on course. It was not yet 8 a.m.

I'd choked down half a biscuit and just successfully pleaded with my heart to drop to a rate of 120 beats per minute when the others started saddling up.

"This stretch," barked our leader, "let's really give it a go, lads."

And with that, I drifted off the back until I found myself amid the cyclists who had dubbed themselves the Game Viewing group. I wasn't sure what I'd come on this trip for—from the moment I'd heard about the tour, it had become one of those irresistible but ultimately inexplicable impulses cyclists are prone to—but I did know that I had not traveled eight time zones, to the cradle of civilization, to the very heart of the world, to ride time trials in sand, endure verbal abuse, and engage in a concentrated study of the rear wheel of a bicycle.

The Game Viewers absorbed me into their herd like I was a lost family member.

"We asked that everyone start leisurely, then peter out from there," explained my new guides, Sarah and Casper. This was a bit of hyperbole—given the demands of the mileage and terrain, there were no hapless cyclists on our trip—but the tone was spot-on.

The married couple (on separate bikes) had spent their whole lives in this territory. They cracked jokes and gave us nicknames as they pointed out hidden petroglyphs, ant mounds the size of Buicks, the ten-degree-cooler shade of shepherd trees, and the yellow, powdery bark of fever trees, to which the Dutch mistakenly attributed malaria.

In photos I'd seen of previous tours, bandanna-masked guides, wearing carbines slung across their shoulders like messenger bags, emerged Mad Max–style through the kicked-up dust of the elephant trails.

I asked Sarah where her guns were.

"I think a guide shot himself in the foot a few years ago," she said. "So now we use elephant bangers, a can that sounds like gunshot when you pop it. Besides, the animals have thousands of miles of open country to get away. Guns are false security."

She thought a little more, then added, "And they would only piss off Mugabe."

Later in the ride I would witness signs of Mugabe's irrationality that justified Sarah's caution. As we rode through the most remote stretches of the bush—"the back of beyond," it's called—we repeatedly came upon skin-and-bone soldiers propped against shepherd trees.

The dictator had peppered our route with a military presence that could barely stay upright. The soldiers offered tentative waves, and we would stop. Out of empathy or pity, not threat, we gave them food. They had us hold their rusty weapons so they could balance plates on their pointy knees while we coached them not to eat too fast. Tears ran down one man's face as he swallowed.

I had to look away.

One day we spotted a clean-running watering hole, and without cajoling, taking a vote, or fielding objections, our entire group stripped down and plunged into the cool water. As we lounged, peloton after peloton rocketed by. Some riders shook their heads at our antics.

Others were going too fast to notice us at all.

Bobbing around in the deep pool, washing off layer upon layer of dust—the standard-issue bandannas did little more than keep the grit out of our mouths—we resembled a load of Burning Man refugees dropped in the middle of the bushveld.

Dave Bristow, a travel writer from South Africa, floated near me and said, "We're still ahead of about a hundred riders."

His math seemed suspect. Based on the number of groups that had gone by, I was fairly sure we were dead last. I ran the groups again in my head. I swore they'd all rolled through.

"How you figure, Dave?" I asked.

He pointed at a cairn one of our bikes had partially covered up and said, "Because the last four groups went the wrong way."

Something about his shit-eating grin brought the same kind of clarity to this trip that I'd seen in the pool's water before we jumped in. I leaned back, relaxed, and took in an approaching herd of zebra—a herd of zebra for crying out loud! I realized that I'd come on this ride to find a way to own some of my life's moments again.

As a husband, parent, and working stiff, I haven't fully possessed one of my days, let alone a week, since the end of the 1990s. Some part of it all had always belonged to someone else. This trip had called to me because it would allow me to stay out on trails from first light until the shine of a fat moon guided me, dirty, spent, overwhelmed, and blissful, into camp.

It also took place in a daunting, remarkable landscape that was burning itself into my see-it-all brain. I was going to ride head-up when I wanted and flat-out if I had that urge. I was going to get on my bike the way I used to, with abandon, and, once on it, I was going to find and hold on to whatever passes as joy in a grown man.

But first I had to put my shorts back on and help clear the kudu antelope away from our bicycles.

The stop at Sentinel Ranch was the first time I'd touched pristine, locked-in-place dino bones. Pure childhood heartbreak had arrived the long-ago day I'd learned that the two-story skeletons in museums—the beasts I grew up fearing and fantasizing into *Land of the Lost* scenarios—were actually plaster of paris.

We'd ridden long and hard to get here, pedaling out of lush riparian woodlands on the north bank of the Limpopo River, through blistering scrub savanna, up the water-carved creases of sandstone hills. Standing over this actual, fully intact dinosaur skeleton was like having a piece of my childhood returned to me on that windswept, red-rock vista. I found myself breathless in a way that would have been embarrassing had I not been able to blame it on the climb.

"My mother found this dinosaur," Sarah told us. Her family had owned this land, formerly the family ranch, before Mugabe redrew all property and boundary lines. "It means a lot to us that we can show you guys these fossils."

Some of it surely was exhaustion, but our group was subdued near to reverence. I posed for a photo I later titled "Bikes and Bones." In it, I'm filthy and wired and despite showing the first signs of bone-deep fatigue around the edges, I'm shockingly alive. No one had seen that guy in years, including me.

By the time we passed the big herd of sixty to seventy elephants, they had put up with hundreds of cyclists pedaling by their feeding grounds—enough apparently, to turn their customary bemusement into annoyance. Suddenly, the warthogs weren't the most dangerous beasts on the trail. As our group rolled by, a twelve-thousand-pounder began waving its ears repeatedly and throwing sand in all directions. I was one of the final riders trying to slip past.

It charged.

Elephants can go from zero to twenty-five miles an hour in short order. A documentary team filming our ride caught the elephant's shocking first burst of speed on video, and its deafening roar, and its pause as it seemed to sink down on itself, stockpiling kinetic dynamite for what I felt certain would be a closing stomp of death.

(Bicyclist versus Elephant video link:
www.youtube.com/watch?v=jnUWSSe69YI)

What the video fails to capture is my high pitched schoolgirl screams of terror.

The oft-cited phenomenon of everything slowing down during a life-threatening situation didn't play out for me. I was a blur of thoughtless primal fear until I was well beyond the herd. Then I was conscious only that I was breathing, though in ragged gasps.

Later, the locals would tell me the elephant's behavior was a mock charge, that if the animal had really meant business it would have tucked in its trunk, so as not to damage the vital equipment, and would have led with its tusks. With not a little amusement, they reminded me that the hyenas that had trapped me inside a port-a-potty at camp the previous evening were actually a more formidable threat.

Driven to intestinal dementia that fateful evening by an adverse reaction to malaria tablets, I'd mistaken the hyena's laughter for cruel-minded cyclists around camp making fun of my plight.

When I'd finally come out of the box for a breather, a circle of a dozen eyes glowing in the darkness sent me back into the stench, where I'd managed a fitful, seated sleep against the port-a-potty wall, a little scared but with my faith restored in my fellow man.

The charge might have been mock. My shrill scream was real. So was my joy at being alive.

Following the trails along the Limpopo River and its tributaries, we weaved repeatedly between Botswana and Zimbabwe, sometimes a couple of times a day. One stands out in my mind—one unlike any I'd experienced in all my years of bike travel on five continents. A card table had been jammed into loose sand on the bank of the river.

A matronly woman sat at the table, which held an ink pad and a basket of pomegranates. I approached, and she stamped my passport. I looked around. The trail ended here, then picked up on the other side of the Limpopo. The woman offered me neither a pomegranate nor any information or advice on the logistics of crossing the border. I shrugged, rolled my bike over to what I hoped would be a shallow section of the river, stuck my shoulder through the frame, and waded across.

Later, with the sun hanging just above high sandstone cliffs, we gathered around what Sarah described as one of the largest baobab trees in Zimbabwe.

She told us that while baobabs may look tough, they're papery throughout—a weakness, but one that expands the tree's place in the ecosystem, as its soft innards are easily carved out to provide homes for wildlife during and after its life cycle. I started to feel philosophical, but opted instead, as I often do, for the physical. I peeled a bit of paper off the tree, smelled the exposed wood, studied the patterns made from jutting branches that resembled Popeye's bulging biceps and forearms.

At the guides' suggestion, we all gathered, clasped hands, and formed a circle around the tree to gauge its circumference. There was a moment of silence.

Then Dave, the other travel writer, said what everyone was thinking. "If anyone breaks into a verse of 'The Lion Sleeps Tonight,' we will be forced to lash you to the tree and leave you for the jackals."

I didn't know which thrilled me more—the good company and easy camaraderie of these cyclists, or the idea that there are still places in this world where being eaten by jackals is a going concern.

We were less than fifteen kilometers from the day's host village, a collection of shanties along a dry riverbed where our food and tents awaited. Most of that distance was a short series of rollers backlit by the sunset playing off red rocks.

We raced one another to the river, in light that made deciding what was shadow and what was boulder a fast-moving art form, little acts of faith and bits of skill woven together, the threads that form the tapestry of every good bike ride.

Somehow we made it down in one piece. Pushing our bikes across wet sand in the half-light of dusk, we had just enough in our legs to limp into camp. That was when we heard voices. Distant at first, then gathering and growing louder—joined in song. Then we saw them. The entire village had gathered along the parade route for the finishers, and had remained to cheer us, the last riders, in.

The villagers crowded the dusty path, children waving sticks, women in full dress chanting and singing and fanning themselves, men sporting old Izod shirts and nodding and humming soothing bass lines for each song. Chickens darted by, chased by toddlers. Clusters of teenage boys packed on donkey carts stared at each bike and each rider.

Our group pulled over to hand out hard candy, coins, and water bottles. Brown-bag luminarias had been lit and placed along the path to guide us the final yards. The words of the lyrical Zimbabwe dialect formed a kind of music I'd never heard before. It swelled and surrounded us. It cradled the broken parts of me.

They were singing, singing, and we were listening.

Chapter 3

THE SUMMER
I RULED THE WORLD

In the depth of winter I finally learned that there was in me an invincible summer.   —Albert Camus

Summer is my season.

If pressed, though, I'll confess that fall is my favorite. That's just my Irish heart talking. It can't get enough of the cool nights, the dying light, a blood-red harvest moon setting over a cornfield; the loss of beautiful things.

Just thinking about young lovers holding back tears, vowing to write, fingertips slipping from grasps as the conductor bellows, "All aboard!" It makes my stomach flutter and pitch. I feed on it.

I breathe in loss and longing the way others take in the mountain air. Deeply, pulling it through and circulating fine mists of sweet misery and melancholy to every limb.

It's always the top of the morning for a King of Pain.

The final curtain call of colors as last light drains off the horizon . . . this has a Christmas morning effect on me. I've pedaled the Blue Ridge Parkway watching it bleed red to purple, blue to black.

I've chased similar afterglows over New Mexico's Black Range, and attempted to outrun the first flakes of snow falling across a sunset at dusk atop the Wacash Mountains in southern Utah. All by bike and all while bathing in the melancholy.

Autumn makes my bones hum with nostalgia and my head ache in all the right places.

The bicycle allows me to ghost from town to town, sucking up the longings of humanity from the discomfort of a saddle. I've never been convinced I truly belong anywhere, but I have a pretty good time everywhere.

But it's summer when I'm at my best. A man in his full. This fully illuminated beacon of utility, virility, and warmth. Of course there's an expiration date to every season, and if you monkey with the laws of nature, those laws will come back to bite your ass.

At one point circa 1990, I spent nearly two years in a perpetual cycle of summer solstices, chasing the season from hemisphere to hemisphere and back until I became someone I barely recognized. On the outside I was a gorgeous savage, tanned, fit, and fashionable in an unkempt way: loose white Panama shirt, flip-flops, Amstel Light in one hand and a volleyball in the other. A lazy, let's-be-friends look on my face much of the time and that glow of health only countless hours on a bicycle and the rest soaking up the sun can bestow. Sunglasses if I needed to go formal and a straw hat I picked up in Cabo for when I played dominoes with the old guys on the boardwalk. Along the way, a wire had tripped, screwing up my internal clock something awful. Stoned on sunshine and tropical breezes, it was as if I couldn't completely wake up. Blissed by the reality of walking around in little more than a strip of fabric around my waist,

I was a modern-day mutation of a dark-edged fairy tale—Slouching Beauty. Too much paradise, dominoes, boat drinks, and reggae music makes the most ambitious person sluggish and sloth-like, but I was just too mellow to do anything about it.

Ten years might have slipped by if my Irish heart hadn't rumbled to life, stirred me to action.

I knew if I didn't find a season or two of suffering I might never put myself back into the world. I would end my time a bronzed shell, going through the motions, shuffling around my own private Idaho, adrift in a saltwater universe, self-indulgent and satisfied, running a chair-rental kiosk on a beach in Rio, or mapping the break line with a metal detector when the surf was too soupy to ride.

Years later, I would attempt to drag my family through a winter in Quebec, Canada, without much justification, but deep down I think a part of me was still trying to balance the seasonal scales. It can be said that penance is a lifelong calling. It doesn't care if you're making other plans.

On account of the extra daylight, or a shift in barometric pressure, I come into my own around May. The unofficial start of my summer is always May 11, my birthday. Incidentally, it's also the perfect launch window for a North American or European bike tour.

May is pregnant with promise. I don't care where you are in the Northern Hemisphere, or how long you want to stay gone, May is when you need to pack your panniers and put yourself in the wind, wings up, wheels down, and off you go; see that you bring us back some decent scars and good stories.

Most of my Mays, when it was just me, went like this: bike ride,

summer camp director, bike ride, summer camp director, rinse, repeat. Sometimes I would accept jobs based solely on camp start dates
so I could get in two months of touring before I was due at most
camp kickoffs.

It's how I ended up running Bearskin Meadows Diabetes Youth
Camp. Rolling in, after climbing sixty-five hundred feet on the last
morning of bike touring into the High Sierras, only to be received
by a towering redwood tree corridor that formed the entrance into
camp. A glorious pedal from Canada to Kings Canyon National Park,
down the Pacific Coast Highway, across cow country, up, over, into
Yosemite, back up, out, over, and across the San Joaquin Valley. I'd
managed to swallow a lifetime of adventures during a few months
on the road.

Einstein would have done well to study bicycle touring since road
time clocks in at a different rate than civilian time. It's a law as solid
as gravity that a week in the saddle pencils out to about a month in
an office. Using this equation, I'd been on the lam from the cruel
workaday world for nearly a year that spring.

Of course every mother's son must rise and fall, and I was about
to take a serious tumble. It wasn't until years later that I gave this
particular crash a proper recounting. Sitting around the breakfast
table with the boys, Beth sparked my memory with a playful seemingly innocent statement.

"It's been long sugary road to the green tea drinker your father is
today. Tell them all about it, honey."

I offered Beth the sort of knowing look reserved for people who
have been through something big and unwieldy together and are surprised to come out the other side united and in one piece: soldiers,

schoolteachers, space explorers . . . parents. "It's a cautionary tale, kids, culminating in heart palpitations at a summer camp I was directing in the High Sierras. In hindsight it was arrogant, cruel really, to drink copious amounts of Mountain Dew at a camp for kids with diabetes."

It's one thing to tell my stories on stage, still another to put them on paper, but when I recount my days out loud for my flesh and blood, it resonates as particularly ridiculous. "I was getting about three hours of sleep, chugging a six-pack of Dew a day at high altitude, running around with a bullhorn and engaged in an after-hours tryst with a lovely arts-and-crafts specialist from Amsterdam."

"What's a tryst?" Sawyer asks.

"Type of cracker," Matteo says. "Continue."

"So what I'm saying, boys . . . it was only a matter of time. One minute I'm square dancing the third go-round of the Pata Pata in the camp's grand lodge, next thing, I'm on my back, chest beating like there's an off-tempo kick drum in my ears. Spots in front of my eyes. I'm swarmed by campers and staff. This being a diabetes camp, their first instinct is to jam sugar cubes in my mouth to bring me round."

Three of my four sons are in rapt attention, leaning forward at the breakfast table. Quinn, my oldest, rocks back, eyeing me like he's my probation officer.

"I took a calming breath, spat out the sugar cubes, and like an alternative ending to the final scene of *Citizen Kane*, I whispered, 'Vegetables.'"

Quinn, the budding book and film critic of the family, shakes his head, but I catch the beginning of a grin.

"Okay, the vegetables line might be a bit of embellishment, or maybe we'll find it in the director's cut, but all I know is I went cold turkey on the Dew. We had a ceremony where I poured my stash into the campfire. I believe Mountain Dew actually has flammable qualities. It was like putting out fire with gasoline. After drinking a couple gallons of water and a day of sleep, I was a new man, sipping the camp's diet bug juice and leaving that bullhorn and some of my jangled energy on the high shelf. Now, Amsterdam . . . she was harder to quit."

Chapter 4

TOUR OF THE GILA

I'm just another traveller
On another winding road
I'm trying to walk some kind of line
I'm trying to pull some kind of load.
—Marc Cohn

All explorers are convinced that there is something wonderful still to be found on this earth. I discovered that when the canyon is deep enough, the forest canopy complete, and the desert soundless and still, I can stop time, a moment here and a breath there, and live happily, if briefly, inside it. But the hearts, and the living we did together, equal treasures. Surprising, since I rode for the empty spaces on the map, to put distance between me and the doings of man.

My daily hike up to the Gila cliff dwellings for my wilderness ranger job was half a mile of heaven. New Mexico mornings at elevation are crisp and bright with a sky colored a shade of blue I've not seen before or since. The steady climb runs through a lush canyon of cottonwoods, quaking aspen, and a spring-fed creek that runs clean and strong year-round.

A few weeks in and already the morning hike was an addiction. Being in the shoulder season meant I could sit absolutely still on a log or rock just off the path and be more likely to encounter a red fox, mule deer, or rabbit than a tourist trudging up the path.

As I was deep into my antisocial period, this arrangement suited everyone. I'd worked my way through Ed Abbey's writings the year before and was going to use the solitude to make another pass at the canon.

Rolling up to the monument on a loaded bicycle after two months and several thousand miles of touring was, emotionally, a hard landing. I'd lived several lifetimes between Idaho and the southern New Mexico wilderness. I wasn't ready to relinquish the road, yet. But the visitor center parking lot was, literally, the end of the road.

I propped the bike against the low wall and stayed balanced in the saddle for a good half hour, admiring what would be my home for the next six to eight months: an Ansel Adams wet dream. Eventually, the head ranger came out from a climate-controlled office and circled my setup, taking note of the homemade Ed Abbey/New Hampshire–inspired sign plates on the back rack: RESIST MUCH, OBEY LITTLE! and RIDE FREE OR DRIVE!

He gave the whole operation a little grunt and asked me right off if I was ethically opposed to operating motor vehicles.

"I didn't think there would be much call for driving in the wilderness. In fact, isn't all mechanized equipment banned in the wilderness?"

He nodded. "But you'll be asked to do supply runs into town two hours down the mountain and transport equipment onto forest service and BLM land. And later in the season it's going to get damn cold on foot or bike for daily treks to the cliff dwellings parking lot."

We'd become friends, but in that moment he was "the man" and I was pure punk band chaos on two wheels.

"I know how to drive stick, got a Class C certification, and will do what's asked unless it's complete bullshit . . . but believe me when I tell you I will manage the pedal, or walk to the dwellings the duration of the season."

He gave me a nod. "No doubt." He patted the bike like he approved. "You want to see your quarters or you planning on pitching a tent through winter?"

My quarters had a woodstove, a family of mice, and a small porch to enjoy the million-dollar view. I considered changing my name to Jeremiah Johnson and never leaving.

I noted him struggling up the path with half an hour left before closing. He had to lean on the monument marker for a good five minutes, then lingered in the caves until the last minute. Too sickly for his age, which I put at forty-five, maybe younger. The whole mortal corporation sucking off the processed-sugar teat and fast-food complex is killing us. He didn't engage me except for a slight nod. My job as interpretive ranger was to provide cultural, scientific, and historical information to the public, but my interpretation of this was, *Let's start with a quick head nod.* Otherwise I sunned myself like a horned lizard, read from the stack of books I had squirreled away in one of the kivas, or wrote in my journal, ignoring the tourists unless they did something really stupid. I kept an ear out for when someone was messing around on the ladders because one had gone ass-over-teakettle into the canyon the previous season. Without the ill-fitting forest service uniform, you wouldn't have picked me as the ranger in a police lineup.

Some days I even did my job with smiles and enough enthusiasm that you'd be fooled into thinking everything was right as rain. Truth? I was maybe two long hikes from heading into the hills for good.

Most of my job was stopping yahoos going off-trail to get sacred and ceremonial in one of the pit houses.

The Gila Wilderness is ten thousand square miles of open territory, basically the lower fourth of New Mexico, tempting me to turn my back on the bitter world. Was this ranger job a halfway house before I walked away? These were the dangerous daydreams that crowded my thoughts as the leaves turned and the sky found yet another shade of blue.

I needed no one, nada . . . not the winsome California girl I'd met in Bryce Canyon who'd come to stay with me the first week on the job only to whisk away one morning, and especially not that sickly gent from last night, who was now sleeping it off inside the cliff dwelling. A perfect walk ruined by another tourist on a vision quest Goldilocksing himself in the indigenous culture's main living area.

The likely scenario? He'd hiked back up sometime after closing to commune with the spirits of the Mogollon people or tucked himself behind a boulder and never left. There would be the requisite dream catcher hoop hung up somewhere, bird feathers placed in a circle, some burning of sage in a smudge pot.

I stood there for a few moments wondering why I cared.

Edward Abbey was fond of pointing out that it's not the beer cans, but the highway itself that constitutes the larger petrochemical-era blight on the natural landscape. Using that same logic, it was the parking lot, visitor center, and reinforced switchbacks helping the public find this eighteen-hundred-year-old wonder that did the real damage, not some guy and his eagle feathers.

Sure enough I found a bag of turquoise stones, a Kokopelli charm, and an assortment of other woo-woo props. Only this pitiful bastard hadn't even uncrated them. Just balled himself up in the center of the raked area and went to bed beside a full Safeway bag.

"Hey!"

Nothing.

"Hey," a little louder. "You can't be here!" He wasn't dead. I could hear a muffled, unhealthy snore, broken and ragged.

Maybe he'd taken something. There were no empties scattered about to indicate a drinking session.

I placed a hiking boot against his shoulder, pushed a few times, not too rough in my estimation, but what was wrong with me that I couldn't be bothered to reach down with my hand?

Perhaps the solitude was turning my heart.

He startled, and that's when I saw an urn cuddled to his chest.

Science maintains there are two responses in a confrontation, flight or fight, but science has overlooked a third: the throwing-in-of-the-towel response. My bandit camper didn't attempt to scramble away or form his hands into fists. He simply sat up, tried to get his bearings, took one look at the unpacked bag of trinkets, brought the urn back into his lap, and began to weep . . . rock and weep.

I stood there in my ill-fitting forest service uniform, letting the man fall apart without acknowledgment or comfort, shifting my weight from one hip to the other, like I was waiting for the line at the DMV to move. Finally, of its own accord really, my hand reached

44

out, coming to rest lightly on his shoulder.

"Okay . . . Okay . . . Okay." I spoke in a calming, rhythmic pattern. A memory of my Mom bedside, rubbing my back when I was feverish flashed in my mind. She'd perform this one-word mantra. Something loosened inside me. I bent lower and rubbed in slower, gentle circles between his shoulder blades.

"Okay . . . Okay . . . Okay."

He rocked and held the urn close and let me comfort him. We went on like that until he ran out of steam. When he tried to get up he was rather wobbly, so I accepted the urn, and with the other hand took him at the elbow. Without enthusiasm, he picked up the bag of trinkets. We walked over to the second set of ladders where the rising sun was baking off the morning cold.

I assumed that would be it. Maybe I'd find him a walking stick for navigating a few of the steeper turns down to the parking lot, then it would be back to my books in my federally funded cave. A clean getaway.

Then he had to go and talk to me.

"That's Charles." Nodding to the urn. "His ashes. My Charles is gone." I thought he was going to his knees and into tears again, but he only exhaled a shaky sigh and took the urn back. There was something tender and earnest in the way he handled the container.

"And I'm not far behind him."

Man tells me he's not long for the grave and I don't even know his name? That rocked me back on my boot heels.

I patted the bench beside the ladder, indicating that I wanted him to take a seat. I brought my day pack from my shoulders, unscrewed a thermos top, poured him a cup of hot cocoa. I sipped from the thermos and waited him out. It was a decent wait.

"Joe," I said, extending my thermos as a de facto handshake.

"Dale." He tapped his cup to mine.

"And Charles, your brother?"

A tremendous amount of air left his body with this sigh.

"Chip was my world."

I waited for more. At the last moment he couldn't bring himself to speak, looking down and away instead. A couple of porcupines unable to find a way between their quills.

Sitting in silence sipping hot cocoa, we could have been old friends instead of awkward strangers.

Then Dale got to his feet, still a bit unsteady, but upright.

"Thanks." He handed me the empty cup and started down the half-mile trail to the parking lot.

And I let him go. Closed my eyes and turned back to the sun. When I opened them, his starter bag of woo-woo crap was sitting by the bench. *He won't miss that shit*, I thought, but I gave it a quick rummage to be sure.

Wallet *and* car keys . . . damn. I dropped them into the bag, started to get up, changed my mind and brought the wallet out.

Dale's culinary institute instructor certification, expired. But he was still a member in good standing with several repertory theater groups in Dallas, Texas. A business card listed Charles "Chip" Hill as the executive chef at The Picadoro. A photo of a robust Dale under a stage door entrance, holding a rose in one hand and a grinning Chip in the other. Across the back of the photo, *Chippendales* penned in perfect cursive. I pulled out another card. A membership to something called the Dallas Buyers Club. I flipped it over, then over again, but nothing revealed its purpose.

"It's for experimental meds . . ."

I'd been caught red-handed. My face burned, but he waved off my embarrassment, picking up the picture from the bench beside me as he sat.

"We were together for eight years." He seemed stronger now that he was talking.

I squint-smiled into the sun. "But Chippendales?" I rolled my eyes a little.

When he laughed I could see bits of the man in the photo again.

"The best part? Neither of us could dance for shit."

And with that, a pair of porcupines relaxed their quills.

I flicked the buyers club card against my hand a few times. Dale took it from me.

"Gray market. Might even be working. Been on them three weeks this Wednesday. Still weak as hell, but if you'd seen me a month ago." He nodded. "It was too late for Chip."

On the walk down to the lot I learned they'd met at culinary school. Dale was his teacher. Chip surpassed him in a matter of months. "Such a natural. He was born to it."

And he'd gotten to play out the thread. Working up to executive chef. Driven, eye on the prize, a real artist to hear Dale tell it.

"One day he had an epiphany, simply cut back work so we could have a life. It inspired me to do the same. Took up theater again. He was in the audience many nights."

Chip's "See America" RV rental broke my heart. Driving around the Old West in that gigantic beast all alone. The tandem bicycle racked to the back seemed like a cruel joke. Like getting stood up for the last dance.

My hands went to it, reflexes more than anything. It'd been nearly a month since the last mile of my bicycle tour from Idaho to New Mexico, and the altered state that bike touring puts one in had all but left me: its tempo, the singular feel of each day in the saddle, the next hilltop, the constant rise and fall of your chest in time with your cadence. The ever-changing landscape a promise delivered. A bike lets us outpace any failures, any frailties . . . the bike is to me what the dervish is to a Sufi.

"Chip stoked, I pedaled up front." He touched the bike's handlebars. Hanging on the back of the vehicle at eye level, it felt like a museum piece we were examining on the sly before security could wrestle us to the ground.

"Chip was shorter by all of an inch but he used that to lay claim to the backseat. We knew it was the professional sightseer in him talking." Dale's voice slipped. He recovered with, "Our plan was to rent this RV, hit the road, park the rig at majestic, stupendous, and just damn quirky locations, and cycle around."

Then he went and died on you. I almost said this out loud. We were both thinking it.

Mind-reading, Dale nodded.

"I promised him I'd make the trip if I was able. Spread his ashes somewhere he'd appreciate. But every time I try, I feel spent and useless and . . ."

"You end up sleeping next to a bag of trinkets in a cave."

We look at his Safeway bag at the same time.

"But I can't let go of him yet . . . not until I feel something."

He kicked some gravel. "Me, the guy who doesn't believe in signs, waiting for one!"

The urn is tucked like a football, protected in the crook of his arm.

"What's worse, I haven't put a damn mile on that bike since he died. You saw me! Barely made it up the trail. Imagine me huffing the tandem over these passes, alone."

It should be noted that the eighty-eight-mile loop from Silver City to the dwellings and down through the Mimbres Valley is used for an annual race; Tour de France contenders in the mix treat it as an early-season tune-up. With fifty-eight hundred feet of elevation gain and loss, the Tour of the Gila is no cakewalk. A few years later, as a reporter for the local press, I would interview, among other up-and-coming riders, Lance Armstrong, Floyd Landis, and Jan Ullrich.

I looked at Dale, his urn, his Safeway bag, and made a decision.

"Get the bike down while I lock the gate."

Dale looked stunned. "What?" Instead of pulling the bike off the vehicle like I'd asked, he followed me onto the bridge.

"Look, what you don't know is I've misspent the better part of five years touring the globe . . . by bicycle."

I worked the rack straps like a seasoned sailor casting off from a dock. In seconds the bike was ready to roll with me in the captain's seat. I indicated that Dale should take Chip's old sightseer spot.

"Did you hear? The Cliff Dwellings are closed today on account of biking weather!"

Dale reminded me of a contestant considering the showcase on *The Price Is Right*.

"You'd do this for me?"

In addition to my antisocial period, I wore blunt like a badge that

year. Prompted by a semester of nihilist writers that included Nietzsche, I felt noble sharing exactly what I thought . . . to everyone,
straight up with no window dressing. It would take my Maya Angelou
period, still three years away, to clarify the differences among truth,
a graceless heart, and outright rudeness.

"I'm doing this *with* you, but the ride, well, that's always for me."

I was a real piece of work. I managed to temper it just a little with,
"But the thing is, it's always a good day to ride!"

Despite the fact that he had a horse's ass at the helm of his tandem, he reached out and shook my hand anyway.

"Let me get some helmets, water bottles, and I have a picnic pannier already packed." He chirped laughter. "I never actually believed
I'd use it all again." He was little more than a bag of bones and a
smile, but that smile was carrying him forward.

Dale poked his head out the side window of the RV.

"You don't know how much I appreciate this."

His enthusiasm was contagious. Try as I might to keep myself
walled off, I was in serious danger of enjoying another person's company. That a gravely ill man had more zest—for life, others, and what
lay ahead—than a healthy twenty-five-year-old was still lost on me
in that moment. I couldn't see beyond the fact that these gents had
spent real money on a quality tandem and had kept it in pristine condition. Also, that I was bison-strong after three thousand miles of
fully loaded bike touring, and knew I could pull Dale over any pass
without trouble. I took it as a challenge, not charity.

Besides, I'd only managed half of the Gila Loop by bike so far.
The other portion had been done in a forest service truck, which
was sacrilegious in my book. Pedaling back over those miles was my

only remedy.

I sounded almost festive when I hollered at the RV window, "Don't forget to bring Chip."

The work began just beyond the parking lot. A long screaming hill down to the dwellings on which most tourists burned up layers of brake pads was, in bike racing terms, a second-category climb. And we had no momentum. Just a few pedal strokes on flat ground before the world went vertical.

In a just world someone would have awarded us the king of the mountain white jersey and five bonus points for topping out. I pretended to be LeMond in the 1985 comeback stage, legs burning, digging deep on an unfamiliar bike and working the gears down, down, down, trying to find a cadence that wouldn't blow out my knees or kill my stoker, literally. Dale did not sound good. Dale sounded like a two-pack-a-day smoker less than a mile into the ascent. The devious part of that first climb was its lack of switchbacks. As if the road crew got word that no more blacktop would be authorized so find the shortest, steepest route from the pass to the dwellings, lay down that pavement, and call it a day.

"Maybe . . . we . . . should have . . . driven . . . up to . . . the pass."

Dale was trying to speak, pedal, and fight AIDS at the same time. This endeared him to me so much. A real fighter, but he needed to learn the first rule of Bike Club: Don't *talk* about Bike Club, or talk at all during a climb this steep and brutal.

I answered his doubts by picking up the pace and issuing a primal yelp that echoed up and down the canyon. Then, because I could taste the summit, I also broke the first rule of Bike Club, yelping away a full cycle of oxygen *and* starting to talk as soon as I'd found some more.

"Nonsense, Dale . . . 'member what I told you . . . it's always . . . a good day . . . to ride!"

We leaned the bike against a rock wall and took in a view to rival the Grand Canyon, while I took stock. Dale wasn't dead. Check. I able to speak in full sentences again. Check.

But my wardrobe was a complete catastrophe. Head-to-toe in standard-issue green-and-brown forest service uniform including metal name tag. Terrible fabrics for biking, or human activity in general—long pants with a high chafe index, cotton long-sleeved shirt with a tall stiff collar. All that was missing was the oversized Canadian Mountie–style hat. If we stood at the vista point too long I'd be forced to answer tourist questions.

I contemplated turning the bike around and screaming down the hill for a wardrobe change back at my cabin, but the climb, even for my inflated view of my abilities, had been too much work. Dale was dressed appropriately enough in black bike shorts and a white jersey. A few sizes too big on him now, but a vast improvement over my ensemble. He did give off the hint of a penguin or a maître d' at a fine restaurant, but I was the real freak show.

I commented on the futility of my outfit.

"Hey, I got Chip's bike clothes in the other pannier," Dale said.

Of course they mirrored Dale's outfit: black jersey and white shorts. I changed in the vista point restroom. The fit wasn't bad, too tight but every spandex rider looks like German sausage, it's just a matter of degrees. Standing next to Dale, something dawned on me . . .

"Yes," Dale confirmed, no guile or irony in his voice. "We were keeping with the Chippendale theme." The memories of picking those outfits and living life's full pageantry together must be what had Dale grinning.

"Me and Chip. The perfect match," Dale said.

I thought of the winsome young woman from California and our brief, deep time together in that very wilderness. My stomach felt strange: hungry and full all at once.

"Well, I commend you for not putting your names across the backs of the jerseys."

Dale shook his head. "Believe me, there were discussions. In the end we thought to just have the outfits be the clue and see who got it when we introduced ourselves."

And most mornings I felt ahead of the game if I had on a clean shirt.

Straddling the bike, I turned to Dale. "That was the biggest climb of the ride, but certainly not the last."

Dale stared down at a speck of river snaking the bottom of the canyon.

"You still up for this?" I asked.

Dale nodded. He looked like hammered shit, but a cheerful pile of it. "Does it matter?" Dale paused a beat. "Isn't it always a good day to ride?"

Well played. And we were off.

We found tiny wild strawberries just after pine flats, kept pace with some pasture horses running the fence line near the Lake Roberts Store, stopped at the continental divide marker for no particular reason beyond it being tradition, and pedaled off-road through a field of sunflowers to locate the roadside waterfall near Mimbres. After that first climb it was flat or downhill for much of the morning.

At one point I looked back and Dale had his eyes closed and his head poking out around the side of the slipstream like a dog holding its head out the car window to catch the breeze.

"Pretty nice!" I hollered.

Dale nodded. "Now I know why he liked it back here. I had it wrong with those dream catchers and pieces of crystals placed in kivas . . . all I needed to do was climb into the stoker seat to find him."

I went silent and just let them be back there together for a while. I pumped my legs until my thighs felt like a forest fire and thought about a girl.

We spread out a picnic lunch in a grove of phallic-shaped rock formations. The play of the sun and shadows throughout the day changed the color of the rock from ember to rust and every shade of pink in between.

It was clear that Dale was finding a second wind when he said, "You know what these rocks look like?"

"Yes. Mushrooms," I said with a straight face.

We had a good laugh. After a stretch of comfortable silence, some good food, Dale said:

"This is what I'm gonna miss the most." He pointed at the two of us. "How people can feel like old friends in one day. It's this thing, you know, you can't name or hold it, you can only feel it. We need each other for the world to mean anything."

He was right, of course, but I had to be contrary . . . you know, Nietzsche and all.

"Please . . . all these unstable bags of salty water walking around doing damage at every turn. We're like hurricanes with heads."

I thought that would shock him out of his good mood, but Dale just smiled and raised a victory fist from the checkered picnic blanket.

"That's right, young man! Rage against it! Means you haven't given in yet."

I snorted back. "It means I'd better walk into the woods for good before I do much damage of my own." I took a deep breath. "Trees don't lie and cheat or bulldoze protected habitats. Trees definitely don't hold you close one night then just leave on the next morning's wind."

Dale leaned forward. "Did you ask her to stay?"

I had not.

Dale leaned back. "You know, you talk like a writer."

"I am a writer!" I yelled. Happy to change the subject and enjoying my rage. "I mean, not just inside my head. I sold a novel to the University of Michigan, but they kill-fee'd it before production. But believe me, I'm gonna make some real noise in the world one of these days. If I don't walk away."

"Well, no offense to Thoreau, but going after the girl makes for a better story than sitting alone in the woods."

It's a helluva thing, being taken to school by what was left of a decent man in the shadow of the most famous Penis Rocks in New Mexico.

We were maybe twenty miles from closing the loop when I realized Dale was asleep at the wheel, or the bar in this case. He'd installed blocks for Chip. The plan had been to have the sick man rest his feet on the down tube blocks. But now it was Dale putting them to use at different times during our ride. On a gentle climb into the lodgepole pine forest I felt his weight go slack. His chin was on his chest when I turned. His hands still held the grips. For a moment I wondered if this had turned into a scene from *Weekend at Bernie's*, but he snored once, perhaps to reassure me. I felt his helmet find a home between my shoulder blades. I pedaled on.

Passing Randy and Debbie's property told me how much farther we had to go. It also gave me an idea. Debbie worked for the forest service while Randy worked for himself, growing pot in the basement. It was a point of pride to him that the federal government was inadvertently funding his pot start-up.

On the first night at my wilderness ranger job, Debbie invited me back to the property for dinner. They hid the plants until it was established that I was not a narc sent by the feds, an elaborate bike-rider/ranger deep-cover government informant. They determined this by offering me some grass. As soon as I took a hit it was as though a game-show-winning buzzer went off, doors opened, powerful lights glowed, and I was in the middle of an enchanted forest of pot. And here I thought all those blankets were covering cages of exotic birds. In the weeks that followed I was asked to tend to watering and flipping grow lights on and off when the couple went on camping trips. There was a natural hot springs on the property. *Pot farmer* never made it on my résumé, for obvious reasons, but it was an easy gig with some good benefits.

"Dale, wake up. We're gonna see if we can bed down here tonight."

I got off the tandem. "Stay by the bike. I don't want to spook them."

Dale could barely keep his feet under himself. "Do you know who lives here?"

"Yes. That's why I don't want to spook them, or you won't have to worry about dying of AIDS anymore."

Gallows humor. Dale seemed to enjoy that.

Randy greeted me, friendly, but all Dale saw was the shotgun in his hands. I'm guessing Dale was fully awake then.

We spent a magical evening watching a fat harvest moon work its way up between the pines. Debbie handed out sleeping bags, and after a good long soak and some herbal medicine, we bedded down around the campfire circle.

"You know what's hard for me to take, besides dying of course, but we're all going there . . . it's the being forgotten part." Dale wasn't sighing or tearful. There was a calm as he spoke, a strength in his voice. "All my life people have been telling me to fuck off and die, calling us freaks and sinners and monsters. We've run for our lives and sometimes it's just been easier to hide who we were. But that part is a little death of its own. The insults, Jesus, the insults and when that one guy spat on us in San Antonio, just for laughing together on a bench along the Riverwalk. Just spat on me and hollered, 'There!' like he'd done the world a favor."

Dale went silent for a while.

"But it was Chip who was the favor to this world. And Chip who never lost hope in it. He loved his family even when they turned their backs for a time. He would tell me how he actually enjoyed vacuuming because it let him see textures changing in the carpet. He liked train rides and rum raisin ice cream. I mean, who eats rum raisin?"

I tossed a few bits of kindling onto the fire. "What else?"

Dale let the stories pour out of him then, until Chip was sitting with us by the fire, too, laughing and adding his versions, his essence. After that night, I've always known that love really is stronger than death. And to think their love was a jagged scar to some people. A thing to turn away from, and even fight against. I made another decision.

"Dale. I'm going to tell your story someday. I promise that you guys won't be forgotten."

It was late and Dale was almost asleep at that point, but he came to for a few moments. "I don't doubt you will, Joe. But you won't get the chance unless you keep your feet in this world. You've got so many good years of people letting you down ahead of you . . . but sometimes, you know, they won't."

We spread Chip's ashes at Clinton P. Anderson's overlook, in violation of who knows how many government statutes. I'd put my uniform back on by then, and saluted the sunrise with a crisp snap of my wrist, so as far as the government is concerned, let's call it a wash.

It was a roller coaster without brakes straight down to the parking lot finish line. We nearly overcooked the only curve but managed to keep that tandem rubber-side down, whooping the whole way.

"Look, this Dallas Buyers Club thing might buy me some time, but since I don't have any family left, I talked to Randy and Debbie last night. They've agreed to let me ship them my ashes."

"They're good people," I said.

"You may or may not have moved on before then . . ." He modeled his bag-of-bones body for me, offering a resigned smile. "But if you're still charming the tourists at the cliff dwellings, then same urn, same overlook as Chip's . . . I'd be honored, if it's not too much trouble?"

We hugged it out.

I kept to those cliffs and dwellings for the rest of the season. On a cold morning in April, two of us in uniform and Randy in tie-dye, we sent Dale into the wind.

Then I went after the girl. And we've stayed in the world, together.

And now, as promised, my friend, I've told your story.

Chapter 5

SOUTHERN ACCENTS

I'm learning to fly, but I ain't got wings.
Coming down is the hardest thing.
—Tom Petty

During the spring of 1987, through a general lack of planning and letting life blow me around like a dandelion seed, I found myself running a bike and canoe touring company north of Gainesville, Florida, in the hamlet of White Springs.

Looking back, it was one of the most unfettered times in my life.

What wasn't to like about White Springs? A place that time had passed over. The kudzu fought with the Spanish moss for dominance and everyone else was happy to abide. I encountered no stoplights, signs or impediments of any kind to my forward progress on bicycle, except the occasional family of mule deer, which appeared to intentionally hide in waiting for me as if it were a game. I'd pedal along at full steam only to find deer darting and dashing in front of the bicycle. It became a test of my abilities to weave and dodge and remain upright any hour of the day. I rather enjoyed it. I also enjoyed rent-free living in an ancient, rambling old plantation-style home falling down in all the right places. In the South, as long as the porch is still intact they tend to wave away those pesky structural engineers and carpetbagging renovators. If that doesn't stop 'em, there's dogs out back or a shotgun just inside the screen door.

I lived there by the kindness of my bike touring company partner in grime, Nancy. We'd started sleeping together almost immediately.

She was ten years older than me, which made her all of thirty-one. Our running joke was I called her Mrs. Robinson in private, Nancy in public, and she called me Sid all the time . . . these versions of Sid and Nancy were far removed from the reality of the actual star-crossed rock-'n'-roll lovers, in both lifestyle choices and how it ended so badly (death and murder charges) for them, but we thought it was a bit of cheeky fun. In many ways that year was unplanned Utopia, so it couldn't last. Sometimes to speak about your life as it's happening is to bring it crashing down around you.

So we kept our mouths shut and cooked elaborate meals that featured collard greens, tabouli salads, and fried catfish. We put in three to four hundred miles of road work a week, leading groups on bike up backwoods bayous where the cypress knees hold court, then down the thinnest, most alluring rebel roads in northern Florida. We'd paddle up peaceful, spring-fed rivers the rest of the time.

Gainesville lay thirty miles to the south. The way its college radio station announced the release of U2's new album, *Joshua Tree*, that morning, was by playing it in its entirety. I reclined the touring van's seat and grooved to it while waiting for Nancy to paddle up with the group. We'd agreed on a pullout spot in Micanopy. I spied a no-name roadhouse bar tucked in the woods framed by Spanish moss and live oaks so thick you might have missed the place. A sign out front for Shiner Bock beer and cooked shrimp was nearly covered by kudzu.

I looked at the time, made a decision, left the van, tied the laces of each shoe to the other and put them around my neck. Then I swam, head up, across the river.

I shook off the river like a shaggy dog does to bathwater, stood in the sun a few moments, then stepped up to claim my prize. When I eased into the darkness I could hear the AC working overtime and feel peanut shells crushing underfoot against the dirt floor. Hot damn.

A glorified homestead with iced beer and spiced-up seafood gumbo, perhaps some live music on the weekends. I walked up to the bar and noted, out of the corner of my eye, a swamp rat of a guy with matted blond hair, wearing the hell out of an army jacket bastardized with nonstandard emblems. Jeans, boots, drinking a Shiner Bock at 11 a.m. on a Tuesday. A man who knew something about living in the moment.

"I'll have one of those." I pointed at swamp rat's beverage of choice, and that's when it hit me. That was Tom fuckin' Petty leaning against the bar with his sweaty, contorted cowboy hat pulled low, drinking a beer from Texas. Born and raised in Micanopy, Petty had come back home. The Gainesville radio station DJ had just been talking about the killer show he'd thrown down on the U of F campus to end a long concert tour.

He was off the clock and the map. Hanging in a place that probably made him feel fifteen again. A place where it's likely he played one of his earliest gigs. A moment to catch his breath and wet his whistle in a sugar shack at the end of the road.

Which was a fine idea, except I needed to tell him all about how *Southern Accents* had changed me on a molecular level. How his songs show that you can love the South but loathe the racism and back-ward-thinking parts of it simultaneously. How it was a complicated, bipolar place to spend your formative years, and if it didn't kill you, you couldn't help but come out of here with an artist's soul. I wanted to make him understand that seeing him on Halloween in 1983 had finally given my Springsteen concert experience a run for its money, and his encore performance of "Rebels" had wrecked me for many concert experiences to come.

I turned and looked at him with such intensity he was forced to make eye contact. Yeah, it was him.

Then, in what I'm certain was my last show of restraint for the next twenty years, I simply tapped the neck of my beer against his, waited for that mischievous, signature Petty smile—part sage, part smart-ass—to reveal itself, then I nodded and walked away.

In a quiet booth in the back I could almost make out, echoing from somewhere down the lazy river of time, the opening chords of "American Girl" being struck into existence from the heart and hands of a straw-haired boy in a backwoods little bar.

Chapter 6

MARRYING UP

The world is full of frauds, corner cutters, and outright cheats, but sometimes, due to circumstances beyond your control, you just get in over your head and it's you they're calling out.

What did Elvis Costello once say? "It's nobody's fault, but we need somebody to burn."

Look at Boston Marathon pariah, Rosie Ruiz. Here's a woman who went from being crowned the winner of the world's most famous race to wearing a crown of thorns and character crucifixion when just hours later it was discovered she had not crossed most of the checkpoints and took a cab for part of the race.

Open-and-shut case there right? Not so fast. Could it have been a poor sense of direction and the infamous cab-driving mafia that is Boston's transportation-for-hire industry?

I used to think Rosie was a debased creature until I found myself on the other side of this sort of equation. Now I reserve a little place in my heart for doubt. It's possible that the biggest cheat in Boston Marathon history was simply a victim of that city's confusing layout and impatient, incompetent cabbies. By the time the driver dropped a frustrated Rosie at what she thought was the start, she was only a few miles from the finish. Only Rosie knows for certain.

But I can tell you the unvarnished truth and lay out the facts about the time I became the Rosie Ruiz of the Seattle to Portland Ride, aka STP. It was a five-mountain morning when I brought out our bike train to make the 2.5-mile pedal to the finish-line party in Cathedral Park. A five-mountain day in the Pacific Northwest is one so clear and bright that it affords a panoramic view of tips and tops of five mountains at once . . . across two states and hundreds of miles.

We were coming off our own high as the lead-out bike float and honorary marshals of the Mississippi Avenue Independence Day parade. Our bike touring train was still awash in confetti, Roman candles, colorful streamers, and neon pool noodles. Red, white, and blue pinwheels spun from the handlebars of the Trail-a-Bike, and the Chariot bike carrier was pimped out in strips of colorful fabrics complete with a sound system featuring Grand Funk Railroad and KC and the Sunshine Band. I jammed three hundred pounds of books in the rig. A sandwich-board-sized poster of one of my book covers stuck out the back end of the Chariot like a JUST MARRIED! sign.

I handed out *Risky Business*–style Ray-Bans all round. Pushing the sunglasses up the bridge of my nose, I channeled the ghost of Belushi and that playful outlaw spirit of the Blues Brothers for a few moments.

"We're on a mission, boys. I don't know who it's for, but we're on one!"

I pushed off. We coasted that ramshackle rolling carnival along the bluff with little to no effort. There was talk about taking a longer route, adding a hill or an incline, anything to break a sweat, but I was scheduled to perform at noon so the real exercise would have to wait. Even meandering our way to the party, stopping to see if I could get the sound system working long enough to groove out to "Play That

Funky Music, White Boy," it didn't take us ten minutes before we could hear the finish-line festivities.

I shifted down for the first time that day and upped my effort to clear the little rise. The rest of it would be a screaming descent to the riverfront park.

And that's when it happened. Our bike train was joined by waves of riders who had just pedaled their rigs two hundred miles from Seattle, Washington. People who deserved the cheers, hoots, and applause of family and friends lining the end of the route. Like a salmon fighting against the current, I made one attempt to go against the flow and get out of this sea of cyclists. I did not want it to look like I was part of the ride, that I was muscling three hundred pounds of bike train across the finish line in front of most of them.

But it was no use. We were caught in the slipstream. And nothing about us was low-profile.

Riders to our left and right actually gasped when taking in the length and breadth of my burdens. They made room, hollering out statements of respect and appreciation for what I had not accomplished. Some rang bells; many hooted uncontrollably.

"Booyah!"

"Dad of the year, right there!"

Smiling, I shook my head and tried to wave them off. This show of humility had the opposite effect.

"Jeez . . . there's a second kid on board!"

"Dave, get a load of this!"

"Way to go, man . . . legs of steel!"

Mind you, we had crossed the length of America the previous summer on this same setup. Seattle to Portland is a mere two hundred miles, whereas me and my boys had rolled it over the Rockies, crossing the continental divide six times, managed the roller-coaster-like hills of the Ozarks, taken on the inclines of coal country to the east, and pedaled all the way up to the Lincoln Memorial.

For a few seconds I was conflicted.

Wait, none of that mattered. We hadn't even broken a sweat today. This was all wrong, but before I could end the charade the high school drum corps drowned me out, that and concert-sized speakers blasting, I shit you not, the *Chariots of Fire* theme song.

As we crested the hill people were high-fiving my sons from the sides of the road. Cameras flashed; a group of riders formed a sort of wedge in front of us so the gap created between us and them formed a focal point with our Technicolor float at its center.

Moms held up babies, people put their hands to their hearts, veterans saluted, and family members looked beyond their deserving relatives to get a better look at this spectacle of athleticism and heart. And off to the side I thought I saw the one Native American, familiar to us from the 1970s anti-pollution commercials, a lone tear running down his face as we passed.

The drums, the theme music, kids running alongside us. I tried to make myself as small as possible. But now something was happening behind me that kicked the crowds into another gear. They cheered in the manner one would a rock concert encore.

I turn to find that Quinn has produced a plastic lightsaber and is balancing on his bike seat, waving it at the hordes. Not to be outdone, six-year-old Enzo, who'd learned how to detach himself from the five-point safety harness system somewhere across Missouri, has thrown open the Chariot carrier flap and is standing with one hand holding the roll bar, waving with the other. He's turned that Chariot trailer into a Popemobile. And though she's been dead for years, Enzo has his Princess Di wave down cold.

"Down, boys, down!" I whisper-yell. But it's too late. As we bring the whole catastrophe in for a landing, we're mobbed by well-wishers. It's like a Mexican border town, children trying to sell us Chiclets and dried flowers. The drums build, the theme song crescendos, someone is blowing one of those vuvuzelas you only hear at World Cup matches. Still, I decide I can weather this heat-of-the-moment, caught-in-the-flood crazy misunderstanding, until the ride director comes through the crowd carrying medals.

At this, I hang my head. The only way I can avoid a medal ceremony is to hop off the bike and beat him to the punch. I come in for a big bear hug. In a panic, I offer him some Italian air kisses before whispering, not unkindly, into his left ear, "We have not just pedaled from Seattle to Portland today on that bike."

With this he holds me at arm's length, shaking a little, looking me in the eye, before saying with a proud, booming voice. "It's okay if it took you two days!"

If I've learned anything in this world, it's that if you present a mob, angry or jubilant, with the truth or the show . . . they're gonna take the show every time!

The crowd goes wild! I do manage to avoid the medal but that's only because Quinn, proudest SOB on the planet at that moment, presented his chest for the director. You know what that kid was thinking: *It's about damn time! I spend a healthy chunk of my childhood pedaling around this fine country with my father, rescuing damsels, slaying dragons, and battling dark sides of the Force from a bike, and finally you see fit to throw me a parade and put a medal on me. What took you so long?*

Quinn stands balancing on his bike seat, arms to heaven in a Ray-Ban, lightsaber victory pose, before executing a graceful dismount. Enzo manages to get the boom box working again, they pose for pictures, mini Blues Brothers with their questionable medals while Parliament's "We Need the Funk" causes a little dance party to break out.

At least the lie is contained to a few thousand cycling friends. I manage to roll the bike train behind the stage and try to center myself for my show. Put the whole incident behind me and get right with myself. I've been hired to entertain the Lycra troops with stories from the road and inspire them with my accomplishment on bike.

"Boys, could we not wear our medals on stage?"

And that's when the whole thing goes supernova. What I hoped would die a quick death has been picked up by Kelley Day of Fox News. She's with her cameraman hunting for a solid soundbite story before deadline, she knows me from other studio appearances, and she must have heard about our entrance.

"It's the Metal Cowboy . . . and his little boys!" She points where she wants the cameraman to stand. "Hoist one of 'em up on your shoulders, Joe. This will only take a minute. In three, two, one . . ."

I would love to tell you that when that little camera light went from red to green, I found the character and courage to set the record straight, that I felt shame and a measure of guilt and confessed my sins to the tristate viewing audience. Instead I channeled my inner Bill Clinton, felt a blanket of calm and peace wash over me. I knew what is, was, and always would be. I felt in control.

Kelley nailed it on the first take. The cameraman worked his lens slowly across the length of the bike train to settle on us—Enzo at my hip and Quinn on my shoulder holding that medal up for the camera—while Kelley asked, "Cowboy, how does it feel to have pulled all this . . . precious cargo, all that way?"

I imagined the piece airing with graphics showing our route and the ticker tape scrolling, "Dad pedals hundreds of pounds of bike, boys, and books from Seattle to Portland."

What I said next, while technically not a lie . . .

I took my time, gave Kelley a confident, warm, road-weary smile, I may have even winked at the camera, I know I gave a nod, and in a voice that had more than a little Bill Clinton hospitality twang to it, I said,

"I'll tell you, Kelley, it feels like I just left my doorstep ten minutes ago."

Another ring in Hell may have to be added for me, but you can't throw that sweet changeup at me and think I'm not going to swing. Back home, I decided to use the events of the day as a teaching moment. I put on Warren Zevon's "Lawyers, Guns and Money," got out the dictionary, and called Quinn into the study.

We looked up the word *fraud* together. He got it. "Like playing make-believe."

"Yes, you could say that, but when adults do it they have two career choices. Making license plates at the local prison, or presidential candidate."

He went to bed in his medal, so here's hoping it sinks in over time. I relaxed, but that didn't last. I realized with a sick certainty that the evening news was about to come on and the only real jury of my peers who mattered, my wife Beth, was upstairs within reach of a

TV remote. I put more effort into the run up two flights of stairs than the whole day of cycling. God love her, when I arrived in our bedroom she was reading a book the size of *War and Peace* and the TV was off. I slid across the comforter, palmed the remote, jammed it under the mattress, and marveled, not for the first time, that I had wed so, so far above my station.

Chapter 7

UNDER THE CAP

Without obsession, life is nothing.
—John Waters

We do things in life, a lot of things, because we don't know what else to do. That's how, during the summer of 1977, I found myself pedaling every cobble brick of South Tampa—from Howard Street Food Market to the Kennedy Boulevard 7-Eleven, from Little General Food Pantry on MacDill Boulevard to U-Save Grocery at that fucked-up five-point corner near the library, all on a freewheeling scavenger hunt for bottle caps.

Coke's plan was for the good people of America to drink significantly more of their specially marked products in search of bottle caps. Peel-off liners featured each state in the union, fifty in all, though Texas was every other cap and New Mexico was beginning to feel like Ahab's white whale. Collect them all and you'd receive a limited-edition T-shirt. Images of Idaho's capitol building or Georgia's official bird made them easier to spot when I went fishing in the bottle cap catch baskets attached to the ends of convenience store coolers. See, we didn't drink brand sodas, just knockoff crap my dad found on sale, so I had to go on the hunt.

We were outliers, definitely not part of Coke's sales strategy.

"Go ahead and take all the caps, kid, if you're just gonna keep coming in and rooting around the bins like that."

Everything changed that day. What began as an excuse to ride my bicycle the length of South Tampa and back again every day of the summer, took on a larger mission.

We might get our T-shirts before the beginning of the new school year. Fourth of July holidays were out of the question given the four-to-six-week delivery time, but back to school was definitely in our sights now. I was hunting caps for three siblings, two best friends, John and Jon, and my sister's best friend, Jane. Jane's family bought the specially marked bottles of Coke on a regular basis. She's the one who secured official game maps for all of us, and a few choice state caps, like North Dakota and Rhode Island. Until now, she called the shots. The rest of us came from cut-rate-soda families—Shasta at best, store knockoff brands as a rule, and always cans, bottled soda of any brand being 20 percent higher.

We'd take shifts asking my dad if he would pick up specially marked bottles from any of the Coke family: Sprite, Mr. Pibb, Fanta, even Mountain Dew's wimpy third cousin from another marriage, Mello Yello.

"Sure. Did you see them priced below Shasta or something?"

Shoulders would slump and we'd go back on the circuit, canvassing floors below bottle return carts and searching the ground around vending machines. No one had thought to ask a clerk if we could just make off with the contents of the entire collection baskets.

"Twist the container to the right and it will come off the hook in the back." I must have looked at him like he was letting me clean out a vault.

"Just don't let any of the soda residue spill on the floor, 'cause I'm not cleaning that shit up." He tapped a cigarette on the counter. "And don't half-ass it on for the next customer or your cap-hunting days in here are over." His grin was one after-work beer away from a sneer.

I took my proposal to six more stores. Only 7-Eleven turned me down. (Later, we'd work in pairs and create diversions while hoisting the bottle cap dispensers and pouring the messy contents into backpacks. It's hard to charge twelve-year-olds for shoplifting used bottle caps, plus it was 7-Eleven, so fuck those carpetbaggers.)

It never felt as good as the first time I pedaled up my driveway balancing a huge cardboard box across my front handlebars. The box full to the brim with bottle caps. I spilled the spoils across a ragged throw rug that covered oil stains in the garage and stepped back, nodding and tapping my chest like a roughneck who'd just struck oil . . . sickly sweet corn syrup oil. I'll never forget the sound those caps made when you ran your hand through them. Everyone gathered around, Steely Dan played on the radio while we worked the pile, calling out states found, getting really excited when an Alaska or Hawaii surfaced, not because they were that rare, but each closed out a separate part of the map. Everyone had Texas already, but we kept a surplus pile just in case.

Something had definitely shifted. Jane gave me a look that made my stomach flip. She was two years older and wore AC/DC tank tops.

In that moment I became drunk on the power of the caps.

I approached the local vending machine guy when he pulled up to the Jewish Community Center poolhouse. Came right out and suggested I do a ride-along so I could pour all the baskets into my cardboard box. I was never without the box by then, though it was showing some age on the four lids, and had dried soda stains everywhere as well as permanent grease lines where it had repeatedly brushed against my bike chain.

His answer was refreshingly to the point. "Fuck no!"

Then he spat on the ground, which would have been uncalled for, except that he chewed tobacco.

"Think I'm losing my job letting minors ride in the truck?"

He looked us over. "After those fifty-state promo T-shirts, are you?" He offered a derisive laugh. "Like 'the man' needs more free advertising."

He rolled an empty dolly back to his truck. We followed.

"Look, if you bike fast enough to keep up with this part of my route, you can have the caps . . . but I'm not waiting for you, and I'm only keeping the machine doors open long enough to load and go." Tough talk, but I noticed him slowing at some of the intersections, and offering a tight little grin when we'd catch up to him in time. Forget all those training articles and high priced clinics: if there's a better fitness program on or off the bike, I haven't found it.

I guess when you move cans in and out of machines all day, anything that broke it up a little was welcomed. For three Tuesdays, John and Jon and I chased that distributor truck from Davis Island to Gandy Boulevard. He gave us a couple of sodas with cosmetic issues to the bottles, and let us sit on the tailgate in the parking lot of The Colonnade Restaurant. Maybe it was all the mad-dash bike riding, maybe because I was drinking actual Dr Pepper from a blemished bottle rather than a knockoff Dr. Skipper out of a can, but I can still taste that river of pop running down my throat.

"Got a new route cross-town starting next week." He pulled the roll doors down on the side of the truck. "Hope those shirts are worth it."

I ran my hands through the sea of bottle caps. It was the first time I suspected that the shirt was beside the point. After everyone headed home from a sorting session, I'd find myself dividing discarded caps into brands and colors and product lines. Hell, I was subdividing by the patterns of the lip ridges.

But consciously, I wanted my shirt more than ever. We all did. Say one thing for a pack of middle school kids, when they want to work as a team for a common goal there's nothing like it. Communism would have swept the planet if no one aged into their late teens.

We could taste victory. The manager at U-Save had unearthed a pallet-sized discard of Coke-specific bottle caps. Knowing the lay of the land, he approached my dad, who brought them home in the back of his Mustang but forgot all about them until I was sent out after dinner to unload a case of root beer Shasta. It was float night.

Calls were made, the usual suspects assembled in the garage. Root beer floats and Supertramp music gave it a festive vibe. There were so many states in that one box that I felt a little dirty. John and Jon kept calling out "New Mexico!" and tossing to whomever still needed one. In this heady atmosphere, I experienced my longest patch of déjà vu before or since.

Everything, the music, the sound of the caps being stirred, the summer light still above the horizon at 8 p.m. and pouring through the cracked window of the garage clubhouse: It all glitched and doubled back in my brain. I knew which state brother Tim would call out next (Delaware) and that it would be my sister Jen who'd ask for it. And I knew I would look up from my map and see Jane's breasts, left and right, free-ranging below her Zeppelin concert tee. On exhibit from only my vantage point. This was more than enough to short-circuit my twelve-year-old brain, ending the déjà vu.

It's not possible to stop time, but at least I got that moment twice.

And the shirts were ours well before the Fourth of July. Over the dregs of our root beer floats we read the fine print for where to send in completed maps. Lots of hoots and hand slapping when we discovered that Tampa was one of Coke's bottling and distribution hubs. Shirts could be redeemed in person during business hours on Tuesdays or Thursdays. It was Wednesday night.

Sometimes you're golden.

For everyone else the carnival rolled up and left town. There were several days when we wore our shirts in unison, looking the part of some Coke-sponsored Disney performance group that had lost its way and ended up at the mall. But fire engine red really isn't anyone's first choice in a T-shirt, unless you're a preschooler or work as a clown on the bullfighting circuit. Needless to say, we were on to something else by the weekend.

Except me. Not the shirt; I was back in my Fonzie T-shirt before the rest of them. It was the caps, I couldn't quit the caps. I'd been storing them behind the garage until recycling center day. But when that day came I moved six heavy boxes of bottle caps into the recesses of the clubhouse. Were I a third-world refugee, someone with grit and imagination, I would have created recycled art, toys—windmills and robots, or mosaics perhaps, matted to burlap from all that metal and color.

Instead, I went back on the road, gathering more and more caps for no reason whatsoever, beyond just feeling good to amass; it felt, well, like America. When some of the boxes suffered a roach infestation, I endured, pouring them onto a huge tarp in the backyard, hosing the shiny mountains clean, and repacking the entire abomination. My obsession had been brought into the light of the dog days of August. I actually felt proud. I didn't care who knew. I talked up estimates of the collection totals at the dinner table.

"You couldn't give the dog a hose-down while you were at it?" My dad's only comment.

I knew it was leading nowhere. I consulted *The Guinness Book of World Records*, but under "Largest Bottle Cap Collection," there was great big nothing. Still, it brought me simple joy. Even when I had to toss a sleeping-bag-sized sack of caps into the street to avoid a nasty car-on-unicycle collision, I wouldn't admit the futility of the endeavor. Yes, I was so far gone I was making my rounds, the close-in ones anyway, by unicycle, a Charleston Chew in one hand and an oversized satchel in the other. I was a live-action cartoon character at that point. And no one put a stop to it.

Early one Saturday in October saw me loading the car full of cans and bottles . . . and my bottle cap collection. This was not done under duress. The levee broke where I was weakest. The night before I'd come around the garage behind Jane and Jen. They were taking in the mountain of caps I'd piled against the wall between the washer and dryer—about 25 percent of the collection, at best. Something made me hang back.

"That's . . . that's just sad," Jane said. "You sure he's not doing anything with them?"

"Nope! At least he did something with all those jigsaw puzzles, remember? Mounted scenes of autumn in Vermont and boats in Iceland on cardboard. Covered the den with five hundred thousand puzzle pieces . . . he wanted me to let him hang some in my room, but I told him to get lost."

Jane stepped up the pile. The vibration caused a shimmering little avalanche. My sister followed her.

"Prussian roaches got into the puzzles, ate the glue he used to mount them. We kept hearing something chewing in the dark and pieces falling off the walls. It was a nightmare."

Siblings can be cruel.

Jane laughed. "Maybe he's got, like, a condition?"

But the older girl next door? Nobody crueler.

I fell from a high place that evening. The top of a mountain of bottle caps, and no one heard me hit bottom . . . only the jagged little edges of caps to break my fall.

Dad's recycling trips were not rooted in the tradition of dignified environmental warriors—the John Muirs, Rachel Carsons, or Barry Lopezes of the world. Strictly about additional beer money, getting over on the man, and a noble-sounding excuse to get out of a noisy house for a few hours. I was a special guest he would allow this one time. There were still two boxes of caps in the driveway, but the car couldn't take any more. As it was Dad had bungeed six heaping bags of crushed cans to the roof of the Mustang to make room. Any reason Dad, former Coast Guard, could find to tie, strap, or bungee shit to the roof put him in a good mood. You'd know this because he'd call you Tiger or Champ.

"I'll take them next time, Champ."

I'd put on my Bay City Rollers T-shirt that morning. Sporting the limited-edition Coke T-shirt would have made more sense, but it was so limited it had turned pink, then nearly white before disintegrating after the third washing.

Right off I could see why Dad liked the dump. Once you got past the sickeningly sweet smells and the legitimate fear that even a small percentage of the billion gulls might swoop down and Hitchcock your ass, it was peaceful. You could make out sailboats on the bay between the mountains of garbage, and the recycling section was upwind.

Dad spoke with one of the guys in gloves and a hard hat. They acted like old friends. After a while they came over to me.

"Ben's gonna let you have a look at the largest bottle cap collection in the world. He'll add yours to it later."

I could have acted disenchanted. I could have pointed out that I wasn't a child, that I knew most municipalities in America had their own world's biggest bottle cap collections. Instead, I took the hard hat and the hand Ben offered, shaking it the way my dad taught me, and gave my father a real smile before climbing the ladder past the AUTHORIZED PERSONNEL ONLY sign.

What got me was the sound. A sea of caps circulating slowly in a huge trough. It struck the same note as when I'd run my hands though the caps in the quiet of the garage, only amplified.

"We move them around like that with just a touch of water pumped in so any excess liquid and debris will drop through the screen at the bottom." I heard what he said, but preferred to believe he was telling me they moved them around because they also enjoyed that lovely sound. Come on. Listen to that.

We leaned against the fencing that kept some moron from jumping in and stayed like that for a while. I closed my eyes. When Ben turned away to say something to Dad, I produced a bottle cap from that useless little pocket inside the pocket of my jeans. I'd forgotten it was there. My safety cap and lucky charm kept in hiding early into the hunt . . . I'd planned to sacrifice it if anything tragic happened to Jane's map.

I let New Mexico drop into that vast river of caps.

On the ride home my dad looked over at me. "That place is something, isn't it. Did you get a load of all the great stuff Ben pulls out for the salvage pile?"

I nodded. "We throw out so much stuff when it still works."

I said this mostly to wind my dad up, a guy who would duct-tape the split soles of my tennis shoes together until back-to-school shopping rolled round. But I really *had* been thrown off by the collection of amazing stuff Ben saved from the crusher.

"Was that stuff collected over the summer, or just this week?"

"Try in the last day or two." He hit the steering wheel with the palm of his hand. Not volcanic anger, it looked more like a motion of frustration, helplessness, resignation.

"We want every damn thing . . . but when that isn't enough we gotta make room for more." He started to say something else, then nothing. I was little surprised realizing he didn't need to.

Dad pulled over at Howard Avenue Food Market. He came out carrying a hot-off-the-press Cuban sandwich for us to split, a premium beer for himself, and an honest-to-goodness name-brand bot-tle of Dr Pepper for me. He kept these goodies in the bag, saying he knew just where go to eat it.

"What say we drive out to the airport at the end of Davis Island, watch some Pipers and Cessnas land and take off?"

I made an exaggerated show of satisfaction tossing back the last swallow of my Dr Pepper only to realize my satisfaction wasn't faked. Dad threw a few rocks into the water; another Cessna touched down and took back off ten yards over our heads. The moment was per-fect. He nodded over, smiling.

"Yeah. But it's back to Shasta come Monday."

We do things in life, a lot of things really, because we don't know what else to do. I still don't know why I kept collecting those bottle caps, but I'm forever grateful that I chose that day to trade them in for some unscripted moments with my father. It's not possible to stop time, but you can collect the best bits of it between your ears.

Chapter 8

WHAT WOULD JESUS PEDAL?

A trickster does not live near the hearth; he does not live in the halls of justice, the solider's tent, the shaman's hut, the monastery. He passes through each of these when there is a moment of silence, and he enlivens each with mischief, but he is not their guiding spirit. He is the spirit of the doorway leading out, and the crossroad at the edge of town.

—Lewis Hyde, *Trickster Makes This World*

It was going to be a quick out-and-back. Me heading up the bike train with my boys lounging comfortably on a Trail-a-Bike and in the bike carrier. My friend Pat riding his lighter-than-air rig, a carbon-fiber frame blessed by the pope in a secret wind tunnel testing facility outside of Rome.

Be it known that parenthood reduces the carefree cyclist to a glorified pedaling taxi service, but I'm not complaining, banking instead that I'll live longer or, at the very least, expire with exquisite calf muscles and the knowledge that I didn't drop dead at a desk. I have lived more of my days outside than in, and most of those in motion.

Pat's sense of humor is as dry as a five-dollar martini, which is why I like to ride with him. That, and Pat's not psycho about racing me everywhere just because my byline appears in wide-circulation sports magazines now and again.

He must get a kick out of our cruiser rides, since we're often going nowhere fast with the burden of my generation in tow. Sometimes I push it just to see him break a sweat keeping up with three hundred pounds of bike train, but we never contest the miles for very long; that's the important thing.

We were pushing for home that morning because I'd just remembered a proximity birthday party we were obligated to attend. What does it mean when I speak of proximity friendships? Those people, often Salt of the Earth folks, with whom you have nothing in common, save for similar addresses. By virtue of location, and one innocent wave on move-in day, a semi-uncomfortable relationship has been allowed to fester.

Soon as we coasted into the drive, Kitty and Stan hauled us in like game-show hosts. Pat tried to excuse himself, pleading no gift, no invite, no mas, but I would not let him leave me. For my part his presence would turn out to be that of a lighthouse during the perfect storm. You see, Kitty and Stan are WWJDs filed in a category so far beyond inappropriate, I'm at a loss as to where to place them.

WWJD is a branch of religious therapy that poses the question, What Would Jesus Do? Taken at face value, this works just fine for large ethical dilemmas on the scale of Would Jesus bomb North Korea back to the Stone Age? Would Jesus sleep with his boss's wife during the Christmas party? and so on. These are softballs for the big Kahuna on the cross. But as with Tabasco sauce and karaoke night at the local bar, a little is almost too much. Jesus as your personal referee; fair enough. But I think it's safe to say that when you are asking your personal savior which shoes go with that blouse, you've ridden the whole thing right off the rails.

What struck me as odd was that featured in the center of the formal dining room table were two massive birthday cakes, decorated to look like matching Bibles, but one of the ebony shade and the other ivory. After the candles were blown out and my boys had a piece of each in front of them, I waded in . . .

"Never pegged you guys as a family of sweet tooths."

"We're not," announced Kitty. "As I'm sure you know, garbage in, garbage out. It's another wicked temptation and a test of one's weakness, but we make an exception on holidays."

I wanted to tell her she's confusing Jack LaLanne for the gospel, but then she rolled out the big guns.

"We just couldn't decide on a flavor so we asked ourselves, *What cake would Jesus eat?*"

Pat began to shake his head. I caught my friend's eye and gave him a pleading look that said, *I've gotta live and ride on this street so hold it together for me . . . Hold it together, my man . . . because it only takes one disenfranchised neighbor with an Old Testament sense of justice to back over me with their SUV. Pat, ask yourself, What would Jesus do? I say Jesus would keep his holy-rolling mouth shut.*

"We were reading scripture."

"King Solomon?" I ventured.

Stan looked impressed, "How'd you know?"

"Lucky guess."

Most of the party guests were sporting bracelets and necklaces showcasing the letters *WWJD*. Why hadn't I noticed this before? Kitty slid another space-shuttle-sized piece of chocolate onto my oldest son's plate. Quinn's expression was that of a lottery winner.

"Still," she mused. "I have to believe Jesus would prefer the lemon cake."

I was gonna say something about angel food, and Pat confided to me later that he had a comment about spice cake at the ready. But my eyes continued to implore my friend to stay mum; my heart and head wanted him to unleash on them, but my survival instinct was too strong. "These people own dogs, Pat."

He took a deep breath . . .

"Pat, Pat, Pat. Ask yourself, what would Jesus do . . . to protect his disciple, Joe?"

But Quinn beat us to the punch. Through a mouth full of cake, his lips covered in chocolate icing, and with no guile or intellectual aggression, he trumpeted, "Hmm boy! That Jesus doesn't know what he's missing!"

The room fell silent.

That's A-list comedy, son. Forget that no one but your uncle Pat and daddy are busting guts with laughter. Forget also that for the foreseeable future Stan and Kitty will most likely release the hounds at the sound of my passing freewheel.Comic gold. Wrong room, but well played.

We were miles down the road, both boys sleeping off the sugar crash in the bike carrier. Chocolate-covered smiles revealing a moment of childhood sloth and privilege. I can pick up the pace when they drift off. I do some of my best parenting (and fastest cycling) when my children are unconscious.

Out of the blue, Pat leans in with this:

"Joe, something's been bothering me for the longest time."

And so it's going to happen: Pat's about to break my rule of keeping friends and work apart. I flinch for a discussion about seat height, achy gonads or hand numbness on long rides, what to pack, which chain lube is shit and which is Shinola.

"I just want to know . . . what bike you think Jesus would pedal?"

Ah Pat, you crazy, beautiful bastard. We'll still be riding together!

I have a good mind to print Pat up a T-shirt I saw in Perth, Australia once—modeled by a Vespa-revving, bodybuilding Australian Scotsman wearing the hell out of it. I believe he'd made it himself. IN CASE OF THE RAPTURE, I'LL BE OFF LOOTING THE HOMES OF THE RIGHTEOUS!

As it happened, I did have the answer to Pat's question.

"For the record, Pat, Jesus would pedal a thirteen-seat tandem, with Judas slacking in the rear."

We spun our freewheels in unison and pondered the truth in this assessment.

"You mean, not pulling his weight . . . mostly likely counting coin back in the Chariot carrier?" Once you get Pat started, well . . .

But how can I be so certain that really is the big man's bike preference?

Because I asked them . . . the experts. And it turns out Stan has a pretty good sense of humor. He appreciated the Judas references in particular. Kitty, not so much. All fun and games until Kitty decides to release the hounds one of these days.

Author's Note: This story is not a dig on organized religion, but a shot at people who take something—helpful or otherwise—way too far.

Chapter 9

RETURN OF THE NATIVE

I want a good life
With a nose for things
A fresh wind and bright sky
To enjoy my suffering
—Wilco, "Ashes of American Flags"

I decided to return to the scene of the crime. I grew up riding a bicycle in Florida in the 1970s, and know beyond a doubt that I'm lucky to be alive, in the way people are who attended Woodstock, rushed for California gold, marched on Selma, or laid the country's first railroad tracks. If that sounds like hyperbole, you haven't spent enough time in Florida.

To be inside something as it's becoming, something organic and ad hoc, dangerous and beautiful . . . roads being paved just beyond my front wheel, often the blacktop still drying as I'd blur by stunned work crews. Bike lanes no more than a pipe dream sparkling in some advocate's eye. Boats on trailers and RVs passing without as much as a tap of a brake light. Three-foot rule? I was lucky to get six inches.

Horns blaring in my direction the way cops fire warning shots. I was never more than a slick wet patch or a slotted drainage grate from the ground. Wind, lightning, and cul-de-sacs, oh, the dream of suburbia, where you could lose hours of your existence puzzling your way out.

Imagine riding inside a pinball machine. It made me hard, confident, and trigger-finger-fast, but only because I knew no other way. I had to ride. I needed to ride, even if I had to steal each mile from a deep place.

The flip side, bikini top girls catcalling you on any given ride, postcard sunsets, swimming before, during, and after a ride, year-round pedaling weather, turning your face up to greet a warm summer rain, roads that had no traffic yet. Riding in the moonlight on a back road with salt spray on the breeze and the shimmering tinkle of wind chimes . . .

To be a boy on a bike in Florida meant no limits or rules.

Now, twenty years later, I greet the roads I once tore up and raced around with both fear and longing. I have plenty to live for and lose these days, and while some of the blacktop miles have bike lanes, all the roads carry more traffic, more distractions . . . and if my reactions aren't as quick as they were when I was twenty, this could be a short-lived reunion.

I called up my old friend Greg, whom I worked with for a while in the Everglades instructing at-risk youth at the Last Chance Ranch. I was a kid telling other kids how to live while most of the management around me were showing the kids, by their own corporate malfeasance, how to really get over on the system. It was surreal and rather stressful work.

Three of us, during a month of Fridays before I quit, would push out the jive and the layers of contradictions by cycling from Venus, Florida, to Fort Myers—a mad-dash hundred-mile ride. We'd leave about 3 p.m. and try to beat the storms and the sunset to the coast. When the wind got behind us and we took turns in front, it was the closest to heaven I'll ever get.

One long glorious breakaway.

The three of us working together to catch a phantom lead rider before the finish line. But when an afternoon squall line would roll in off the Gulf, the road slicked up with oil and tar spots, the lightning sparked God's Taser and it was hell on earth.

Not only could we see the lightning, sometimes only yards away, crashing in jagged flashes, but more than once we smelled the ozone, all the while knowing we were the three tallest points for miles. After one very close call, I hollered that I was going to lie down in a culvert by the side of the road and wait for the worst of it to pass over. And then I rolled into the ditch.

I was stunned when they joined me.

The sky was so black it felt like night, until the lightning strobed it to daytime every ten seconds. There we lay, screaming in terror and primal release until we ran out of breath. Then one of us gave the all-clear and, like it never happened, we were back on the blacktop, finding a cadence and talking sports or asking where we wanted to eat at ride's end.

Good times, if you lived.

Greg made the reunion ride but Steve, the third amigo in those Friday fun-house sprints, begged off. More to the point, he told us we were nuts. When pressed, he confessed he hadn't been on a bike in fifteen years but still thought he could whip our asses, then remembered what I did for a living and changed his tune to questioning our sanity again.

"Why would you want to take on that road again. It's a loaded gun. No one lived out there back then. They'd only just blacktopped it when we rode it, hoping all those Boca Del Vistas on the coast were gonna fill up with old people. It's gotta be full of cars now, driving too fast, not paying attention, old people, man. They'll take you out and think it was a gator."

Instead, Greg brought his twenty-year-old son, Bobby.

"Bobby, do you mind if I call you Steve, it would really help me complete the circle of life and memories and the authenticity of this ride?"

Bobby looked at me as if I were having a stroke since the words coming out of my mouth weren't making a bit of sense.

I broke a wide grin. "Just messing with you, Bobby." He visibly relaxed and gave me a *so that's how it gonna be, is it?* nod and smile.

Greg got his bike down off the trunk rack. "Haven't changed a bit, have you, Mad Max?"

Some rides are special because of the company; some are all about the scenery. When it's both you're in rare airspace.

The blacktop was no longer new, smooth, and fresh. Cracks and divots and dips where the soft sand underneath had given way: That's what ruled the day. Grass and road debris littered the edges. We made it more of a tour ride than a training sprint. No rain this time to put us in the ditch, which was fortunate because at our slower pace we spotted more than a few healthy-sized gators sunning themselves just off the blacktop.

Maybe they'd been there twenty years ago, but between the lightning and the primal screams I hadn't noticed. We'd heard of a new hazard to cyclists on this route, pythons. They're taking over the Glades according to a park ranger. I cracked a joke about hoping to bunny-hop one if we found it stretched across our path. He looked at me the way one might observe a frat boy considering some Darwin Award–winning stunt involving garage roofs, hot tubs, and power lines.

When we reached the beach in Naples, I felt more than a hint of cramping in my quads and the faint metallic taste of blood in my mouth. It was foolish of him, but Greg kept dousing Bobby with tales of the glory days of this ride, talking up our average speed and the way we'd kick it into overdrive for the final twenty-five miles to the shore.

When that young buck went rabbit on us at the eighty-mile mark, I only had a second to see what shone in Greg's eyes and another instant to jump and grab onto his rear wheel, or get dropped off the back. I jumped and in five or six pedal strokes I was tucked in behind my old friend. From there, we took up the task of working for one another in the hope of running down the breakaway. He had maybe thirty seconds on us . . . what he wasn't carrying was an extra twenty-five years, but we had experience, cunning, skulduggery, and each other.

Whether we caught him or not is beside the point because for a few hard-fought, glorious miles we managed to slip back two decades and ride wheel-to-wheel and stroke-for-stroke with our former selves. For the record, though, we ran down that uppity little bastard, but just. And the rule back then was, if you made a run for the yellow jersey in the Tour de Gator, and we pulled you back to the peloton, dinner was on you.

Chapter 10

LIVING WRONG

Explore the forests, climb the mountains, bag the peaks, run the rivers, breathe deep of that yet sweet and lucid air, and I promise you this much; I promise you this one sweet victory over our enemies, over those desk-bound men and women with their hearts in a safe deposit box, and their eyes hypnotized by desk calculators. I promise you this: You will outlive the bastards.

—Edward Abbey

"Where's your yellow bracelet?"

Two racers, on a training ride I assume, flank me at the light. We're at the top of the hill. I passed them coming up; this being my daily climb I've become mountain-stage-strong on it even though I'm doing it on a tandem, attached to a Trail-a-Bike, which is hooked to a trailer. Altogether it's me and three sons in tow. If not for traffic laws I'd have been a spot on the horizon, but the red light allowed them to pull even. As we wait for the green the one on my left, executing a decent track stand, rephrases the question. This time it sounds closer to an accusation.

"You're with us for Lance's fight against cancer, right?"

I look at their wrists: Yellow plastic loops are on prominent display. I'm down with that, but what's throwing me into a state of stunned confusion involves guys in that much spandex and wrap-around eyewear speaking to me in the first place. Normally, racers talk only among themselves, like ants in a colony (if you look closely you can make out their antennas). They'll occasionally acknowledge my existence with a slight nod if I happen to be wearing one of my sponsor's jerseys or forget my panniers or several children at home. Barring that, I'm dead to them.

But I did just pass these svelte gents on a grueling hill. Might this have caused a tectonic shift in our lines of communication?

What I want to say to them is, *Hey, if blowing you guys off the back on that hill doesn't count as living strong, I doubt a yellow band of plastic is going to tip the balance.* Instead, I give a reserved nod.

But this is a point in history when you don't diss the yellow band or the man who made it famous and live . . . long, strong, or anything else. The cult of Lance is out of hand. The thing is, I've met, pedaled with, and interviewed Mr. It's Not About The Bike and had my doubts, not regarding his athletic prowess, but about his character.

I stay mute while they look over at my son's naked wrists. Quinn models a shark's-tooth necklace we searched out in Hawaii and Enzo fashions a Pokémon decoder ring the size of Delaware on his pointer finger, but no canary-colored bands of courage.

Oh, the shame.

The racer on my right points at his bracelet, nods, then gives me the thumbs-up.

Now they're creeping me out. A bit too evangelical about their bracelets for a Saturday morning, or any morning, really.

At the time the ubiquitous yellow plastic was on every third wrist in America. If you hadn't seen them you were color-blind or about to walk into traffic due to a complete and chronic lack of attention to the world. Before you stumble to your death, allow me to recap. Lance Armstrong achieved his victory against cancer through powerful treatment and daily hard work, luck, and an ornery Texas death-match attitude. I can speak to his attitude because I once interviewed this young and improving, cocky racer after the Tour DuPont. The kid showed the right combination of brash self-preservation and enough chutzpah to scare the bejesus out of the most experienced racers that day. Cancer didn't stand a chance. But it did change his physical makeup, and seven Tour de France victories gave him the platform to support other cancer victims by creating a foundation that created the yellow Live Strong wristband. With help from Nike, the bracelet was launched in 2004 and became an instant, worldwide success. Money went to research, presumably—and almost sixty million bracelets sold.

An amazing story, which brought profits to Mr. Armstrong, the plastics industry, and yellow dye 7. After Armstrong's fall from grace it came out that, with forethought, malice, and intent he ruined the lives of a number of people who spoke out about his performance-enhancing drug use. He also traded on the goodwill of his foundation to massive personal financial gain and used the foundation affiliation as a shield to help put himself above reproach.

Whatever laws he did or didn't break, he broke the trust and hearts of a generation.

In 2007, I pitched an article to my editors at *Bicycling* magazine titled "Working on the Chain Gang." In it, I wanted to follow a team like the one Lance Armstrong rode to, for a full season, and do an in-depth piece on the doping that I, and everyone within the bike racing industry, knew about. It was lauded as a hell of an idea and dismissed without further discussion. The Armstrong era had ushered in too much money, for the media, for the sport, for everyone, and they weren't about to bite that hand.

But none of that had happened yet. The reason I wasn't sporting the band was because I just don't like jewelry, or accessories of any sort, on my person, anywhere. Hats I like. Hats I would wear, if I didn't look so foolish in hats. Put any make or model on my noggin and it takes twenty IQ points off my appearance. Ball caps are the worst. Pop one on me and I feel the need to chew gum with my mouth open, talk NASCAR, and top off your tank with premium unleaded.

I wear a helmet because of gravity and velocity and other Newtonian laws, but l won't be offended if you look away, it's almost too graven an image to force upon the world. The addition of bracelets and I would be absolutely hideous. My only choice would be to go over the top; piercings, a tall bike, large tattoos, some eyeliner perhaps. Or pull a Liberace—glitter, owl glasses, platform shoes, and rings on every finger.

Other bracelets that I appreciate on paper, but won't wear . . .

Live Wrong

A black, plastic pirate theme bracelet featuring a Jolly Roger skull and crossbones on the opposite side from the words.

This one set off a firestorm of criticism when the more somber contingent of the Live Strong crowd complained that it was mocking their efforts.

Here's the marketing campaign for the Live Wrong bands:

"Finally, a bracelet that reflects our lifestyle! We party . . . a little. We eat red meat. We enjoy a beer now and then. We take risks. We like extreme sports. We paintball, snowboard, skateboard, mountain bike, BMX, and rock climb. We stay out late, get up early, work hard, play harder and we love our lifestyle. We live on the edge, and we aren't going to apologize for it. Does this mean we live wrong? You bet it does. And now we want the world to know that we are not ashamed of our lifestyle! Live Wrong . . . the bracelet for the rest of us."

A bit of cheeky fun but in the end it offered more sincerity and a more honest manifesto than a warehouse of yellow bracelets. A lively young cyclist came up with it after a few too many drinks and viewings of *Pirates of the Caribbean*. He was, in fact, wearing a Live Strong bracelet at the time. The Internet flaming over these playfully defiant bands of black quieted down when it was discovered that many actual cancer survivors loved the celebratory attitude and wore them alongside the yellow ones.

"I never thought anyone would buy them, but as I've made clear, I'm wrong about most things," the creator was quoted as saying.

Others added to the credo, stating, on one blog, that to live wrong should include:

Taking a year off of school to travel.

Showing her you love her with something you actually do or make.

Volunteering as your vacation.

Eating local.

Quitting a job you don't believe in.

Riding a bicycle as transportation within a car culture.

To me these sound like Live Different or Live Well . . . Within Your Means, but I could be wrong. Indeed, the gross national product, which for no good reason we use to measure the United States' economic health, is counting on it.

Live Bong

You'll find this bracelet dangling from relaxed wrists in many beachfront communities and surfing hot spots around the globe. Made from hemp rope and tie-dye or striped with the colors of the Jamaican flag, it predates the Live Strong loops by thirty years or more, though I'd never seen similar phrasing on one until I wandered past a surf shack in Jaco, Costa Rica. The place rented boards and sold relaxation therapy one ziplock at a time. As the employee lit up not fifty feet from the policía station, I noticed his bracelet read LIVE BON.

"Yeah, bra. Someone forgot to stitch in the *G*. Musta gotten distracted." A long, stoner laugh fills the small shack. It's eight o'clock in the morning. Wake and bake.

"Cops don't hassle you for selling in the open?" I nod over at the policía station.

"Pura vida, man. They're some of my best customers."

The light turns green. I allow the bracelet-bedazzled duo to get a good jump on us. I'm about to launch into a lecture/discussion with my sons about the pros and cons of overzealous missionary work when a trickle, then stream, then river of cyclists pedals past. Then more, and more still. Half peloton, half parade. And all of them sporting yellow bracelets, some wearing yellow T-shirts announcing the ride event they're participating in.

My world made sense again.

Those spandex boys weren't crazy; they just thought I'd forgotten to fly my colors. Without realizing, we'd been riding along the same route as a Live Strong Challenge Ride.

The next time you see me, I might be wearing a triple threat of yellow, black, *and* Jamaican flag flying bracelets. A hat, even. Perhaps a fedora.

But don't count on it. If I've learned anything from the rise and fall of Lance Armstrong, it's this: It *is* about the bike, and always will be about the bike . . . that freedom it offers so many, as transportation and health club rolled together, as a tool to combat debilitating injury and the loss of mobility. It's better than Viagra and stronger than the demons inside your head. A fountain of youth, a respite from the workaday world, and the wheel that turns anyone willing to get on one into a child again.

Chapter 11

A SHINING MOMENT ON MOUNT HOOD

That's your job in this hard world, to keep your love alive and see that you get on, no matter what.
—Stephen King, *The Shining*

Pacific Northwesterners did not invent clever names for athletic events, but it was wordsmith worship that attracted me to my first Summit to Surf diabetes charity bike ride. With its catchy name I fully expected to pedal to the top of a mountain, plant a front fork at the driveway of Mount Hood's historic Timberline Lodge, then clip in for a bone-shaking ride, a near-vertical run, some sort of a tuck-and-go-like-hell all the way to the Oregon coast.

Instead, a couple thousand of my friends and neighbors assembled outside a one-room schoolhouse in Welches, Oregon, for fifteen miles of slow going, up and over Barlow Pass, before coasting thirty gentle klicks to the water's edge—Hood River and the "surf" of the Columbia River.

Don't get me wrong, Barlow Pass is a lovely spot on the planet, but it's a far cry from the rarefied air of Timberline—the prize waiting for me at the tip-top of a crooked and steep fortress of stone, something Dr. Seuss might have drawn on a frisky day. Or so I was told. I'd never been to the lodge. If I'm going to rise at the crack of dawn, work those pedals in a way that resembles a gerbil on crack, play my gears like a concert pianist performing Rachmaninoff, then at the very least pay my efforts with a million-dollar view and architecture listed on important registers. Not to mention that while Barlow Pass pedaling may sound like a formidable accomplishment, when I found myself drafting behind a school group of sixth graders hardly out of breath, drastic measures were called for. Someone throw me a testosterone life preserver, stat, then point out the turn for Timberline.

Two bike lanes diverged in the Oregon woods and I took the one less pedaled. I took the one that held the promise of hypothermia, blowing rain, and icicles forming on one's chin at the tail end of July. My rescue came in the form of a small addendum to the official Summit to Surf brochure; something I'd missed until it was nearly too late, a last-minute Timberline Lodge option for those hearty souls who find pain and suffering their stock in trade. With a gleeful wave, I bid farewell to the elementary school set. Peeling off their raggedy back wheels was a sort of liberation on par with graduating from the kiddie table at holiday dinners.

Once away from the crowds of casual riders—folks in their funny hats, theme music, bells, event tees, and dusted-off garage-rafter bikes—I searched for a rhythm I could live with as the earth began to tilt up. I knew to pace myself on what would be my lonely flight of folly to the top of the world.

Only in Oregon, though, can a man commit such a brazen act of independence on two wheels and find himself followed into the breach by a rowdy armada of blue-blooded cyclists, fellow inmates from the Lycra monkey house looking for a challenge that might very well put some of them on the evening news or in the hospital.

"Heard they're offering medals to those who make it to the lodge." This from a man twice my age who had apparently given up all signs of body fat the way others kick hard-core vices such as heroin or hookers. And he was about to kick my ass off the mountain if I didn't pick up my pace.

I nodded to conserve energy in case he made a run for it mid-sentence.

"Only for those who make it back down again," added a serious young man in front, probably a triathlete using this as a training ride. He shook his head as if the concept of medals was laughable.

"Medals? Baah . . . There's hot chocolate and homemade pie at the Timberline turnaround rest stop," the old man's sidekick said, his son perhaps judging from body type and crooked grin.

Now, I do likes my pie, but the way I was sweating, hot chocolate just seemed silly. A medal, though—that didn't sound out of proportion. I fell in behind them and had a look around.

I counted eight of us in all. A pair of pretty boys—the sort ready at a moment's notice to step in as *Bicycling* magazine cover models. These posers would be the first to drop when the going got tough. Never dress like a Tour de France team member unless you're actually in that race, and never ever ride more bike than you can use to successfully pass others. It's a dead giveaway.

The big guy midway back in the pace line—now, he was the one to keep an eye on. Resembling a whiskey barrel that had managed to defy gravity and mount a bike, his tan lines told the real story. This barrel of Booker Noe rode four or five times a week. Anyone strong enough to pull that much heft uphill, while carrying on a conversation, was a bear.

Don't poke the bear.

The woman using him as a windblock? Poster child for the Pacific Northwest outdoor lifestyle. A peek in her closet would reveal more Gore-Tex shells than cocktail dresses, her bathroom stocked with more Carmex than lip gloss, and her garage jammed with Windsurfers and snowshoes, leaving just enough room to park the Subaru.

I could love this woman, if only I could find enough oxygen to introduce myself.

Rounding out our band of Timberline hopefuls was a husband–wife team on a tandem. Tandem riders fall into two camps: those who wave and smile at anything that moves, as if in training for the Rose Bowl Parade, as if a soundtrack accompanies their every pedal stoke, one featuring classic hits for 1976, "Skyrockets in Flight," Redbone's "Come and Get Your Love," and Frankie Valli's "Oh, What a Night." And then there are those who work for Boeing as structural engineers. The engineers were bringing up our rear, scowling, determined, all systems go.

Every few miles of elevation gained the group access to a new ecosystem. Arboreal forest glistening in the sunshine gave way to subalpine with its puffy clouds and crisp breezes, before handing us off to growing shadows across alpine meadows.

Somewhere between admiring my natural girl's calves and thinking about fine hickory-smoked whiskey, the temperature dropped forty degrees and the rain began to fall . . . sideways.

As underprepared as I felt for this assault of elements, my rear pannier held a trove of clothing options compared with most of my compadres. Only the triathlete and the engineers kept going when the pace line stopped for a wardrobe change. The flimsy windbreakers and thin fleece being donned were laughable, but it was all my fellow cyclists had. I lent a layer to the old guy's sidekick, who mouthed "thank you," but what I chose to hear instead was "hot chocolate." It didn't sound so silly now.

When we caught the stoic couple on their two-seater, they'd managed an in-motion head-to-toe clothing transformation. Mussolini would have been proud.

For another three miles we concentrated on making little circles with our pedals, battling back that coppery taste of blood in the back of throats as conditions deteriorated at cartoon velocity.

"It ever snow in July?" I asked, realizing, even as the words left my mouth, that images of Mount Hood always, always proudly display snow on them.

Whiskey barrel seemed not to notice the icy rain or biting wind, but one of the two pretty boys was grunting and barking, making a spectacle of himself, while the other suffered in silence. That's when the lodge came into view.

I had to wipe my glasses twice before it registered. This being my first time setting eyes on the famed landmark, it jolted me upright in my saddle. Even through blinding rain and wind gusts strong enough to blow a bike right over the edge if one wasn't mindful, the front facade of Timberline released a fight-or-flight burst of adrenaline, mixed with so much emotional vertigo that I had to grip my handlebars and bite down hard not to lose my place in the pace line. Crashing everyone to the ground is considered poor form on any ride.

Something hot and damp danced down my spine.

"Wait a minute, this looks . . ."

Sidekick nodded. He knew where my head was at that moment.

"Here's Johnny!" he howled, waiting me out. "You really didn't know they filmed the exterior shots for *The Shining* here?"

I shook my head. Rain flying off as the stark realization leaked in. Struggling the final yards into the parking lot brought it all back. I was forced to view the film way too young, and every reel of it had left an impression that sweltering Florida afternoon of terror. Mom claims she didn't even look at the title, she just saw the movie poster with all that snow, knew the theater was air-conditioned, and took in whichever family member happened to be in tow. Me.

Later, when questioned by my older sister as to what she was thinking taking me to a Stephen King horror film, Mom pointed out that she was a Florida housewife with four children during humidity and cockroach season. An unkempt ax-wielding Jack Nicholson seemed laughable in comparison.

Now here it was in the flesh . . . or stone and masonry. Scaring the crap out of me all over again.

As soon as we came to a stop something else sent fear through the group.

"Where's the hot chocolate?" someone whined.

Several tables with party skirting stood abandoned beside a locked, darkened lodge.

"Where's the rest of the rest stop?"

Triathlete pointed at a white blob hanging in the low branches of a spruce tree. Upended and covered in mud, the party tent invited anything but celebration.

When Dan Stathos introduced the bicycle bill back in 1971, I wonder if he ever envisioned that funding projects would lead to cyclists behaving in such a manner so early on a Saturday morning. Probably; after all, Oregon rarely tells its people what they can't do in the name of physical fitness.

A murder of crows flew a tight formation over the tables, landing only long enough to pick at the mushy remains of breakfast muffins. I do believe that's when the pretty boys lost all hope.

Whiskey barrel yelled something, but gale-force winds swallowed it whole.

"At least it's stopped raining," I heard when he tried again.

And there it was, the core Oregonian spirit embodied in a rolling barrel of Booker Noe and Columbia Sportswear windbreaker. The eternal optimist facing down ridiculous meteorological conditions. It reminded me of British explorers stumbling about, frostbitten from days on the polar ice, asking only for a spot of tea before it's back into the breach with them. I would do well to emulate the big man, seeing as we had recently chosen Oregon as our final stand.

That's when it started to snow.

Not storybook flakes, sleigh bells, and caroler conditions, but a swirling dervish of chaos. A cold white whirlpool of loathing. I took one last look at the haunted house of my childhood—a regal structure made so wrong by the magic of Hollywood—and headed for the low country as fast as my legs would send me. Echoes of "Redrum, Redrum" nipping at my heels, ice and snow stinging my face.

I assumed everyone followed, but did I take an actual inventory? There was still a bit of East Coast in me that needed to be purged.

In time, I learned the customs of our region, a land where people made eye contact, conversed in coffee shops with complete strangers, and held doors open for no other reason than . . . it's the right thing to do.

Not until I was safely back into the warmth and light, rolling across the finish and into the feed line, did I notice we were a few people short. Tandem couple offered a nod, nature girl held her face to the sun, whiskey barrel already had his plate, the father-and-son team were showing off their medals, but the pretty boys and triathlete: absent. I scanned the bike corral for their expensive rigs: nada.

A woman with a clipboard, radio, and red-ribboned medals came to our table.

"You guys slipped up the mountain before we could close the road. Congratulations." She handed us our medals.

"We had to send an ambulance for two other riders. Hypothermia."

"Who called it in?" I asked.

"That guy."

When we followed her finger, it led right to our triathlete, sucking down a power drink, still in the saddle. As if on cue, he pedaled away, in the direction of the mountain. More than likely riding the course in reverse, back to his car.

You know he didn't take a medal. The only true Oregonian among us that day.

Of course, being a vain little creature in spandex, I kept mine. I did put in a good word so that the pretty boys in the hospital would get theirs as well.

It's another summer. Two roads diverge in the Oregon woods and like a good hunting dog, one that can't stay put on the porch, I gear down and head up the hill for another crack at it. Another chance to leave none of my neighbors behind. The chance at another shining moment on Mount Hood.

Chapter 12

FIELD OF FROZEN DREAMS

Snow is God's attempt to make a dirty world look clean.
—Mehmet Murat İldan

Never again will I whine about pushing my metal steed into a Northwest winter—griping about a chilly little bike trek down to the library, grocery store, or schoolyard drop-off and pickup in January. Slogging my two-wheeled transport into the barometrically challenged elements for St. Patrick's Day party supplies or a misty rain ride along the Springwater Corridor.

Based on the bitching I hear and overhear from my fellow cyclists, few of us realize how good we have it out here. Only a handful, in my estimation, show the appropriate appreciation regarding the flat-out luxury, the absolute joyride that is a Pacific Northwest rainy season by bicycle. That, or maybe we could all use an object lesson in the relativity of suffering.

I went to Iowa one winter. Consider me schooled.

There will be no more bemoaning the many ways in which rain is ruining my morning commute or that, with the windchill factor, it feels like twenty degrees along the river during the Sunday-morning loop ride with my club pals.

You see, I trekked out to the unpromised land one February and came back a changed man—the cycling equivalent of Bill Murray's character reborn in *Groundhog Day*—only the backdrop for my deep-freeze drama wasn't Punxsutawney, Pennsylvania, but Perry, Iowa.

"Cold enough for you?" This became the traditional greeting echoed by every taxi driver, waitress, and desk clerk during my four-day stay in Des Moines, Iowa, as the entertainment for the Iowa Bicycle Coalition Summit and Bike Night Auction (thankfully, held entirely inside the climate-controlled confines of the downtown Holiday Inn Conference Center—love that Midwest buffet tradition, but people, three full troughs of breakfast sausages cannot be FDA-approved).

I could have laughed off the multiple feet of plowed snow along the roadways and icebox temperatures, if not for the fact that I had agreed to pedal as their B-list celebrity cycling author on a weekend ride in neighboring Perry, Iowa. I'm told they phoned Lance first but he was off living strong and warm in the saddle somewhere near the equator. No doubt an umbrella drink sticking out of his water bottle.

Here's the *Des Moines Register*'s quick take on the ride: "About 500 cyclists from around the state braved below-zero temperatures to participate in the 30th Annual BRR Ride, a 30-mile bike ride from Perry to Rippey and back (Bike Ride to Rippey forms the event's initials). With the temperature around minus 5 degrees, negative 25 with the wind-chill, riders pedaled through one of the coldest organized rides in the country."

What that soundbite neglects is that up to three thousand people often turn out for this event, the unofficial kickoff party of RAG-BRAI, the Register's Annual Great Bicycle Race Across Iowa. Cyclists—racers to commuters and everyone else in a thousand-mile radius who decides to dust off a bike that morning—digs out some sort of wheeled contraption to "pedal and party" around Perry. This year most of them stayed inside church basements, gyms, and bars, waving while the stark-raving foolish in search of frostbite took to the wind.

What was I thinking? I haven't been Catholic for several decades . . . and still I can't refuse requests involving voluntary acts of suffering with no good explanation . . . beyond the carrot of "Character Building." I'd rather build a fire over here for potential survivors, thank you.

The facts on the ground felt more like an assault on Everest or a suicide mission than a bike ride. A few miles out of town, those who had thought it would make a great bar tale were already turning around. I nicknamed them "the Mensa Club Contingent." Shortly thereafter we noticed stray winter clothing and bike wheels littering the snow, people doing their best imitations of the Michelin Man in massive parkas throwing in the towel, or "resting" along the shoulder while their lungs thawed out enough to call out for help.

My friends at Bike World set me up on a Trek 520. It was one of the lucky rigs not to have its lube and chain grease freeze, locking up the freewheel like a bank vault. I was sporting no less than eight layers of long johns, multiple River City Bicycle logo winter tights, bibs, and jerseys. Brian Duffy, the editorial cartoonist from the local newspaper, took pity on me, not only lending me an extra ski mask—the one with a name that sounds like an expensive dessert—but also allowing me to sit in his shadow for the headwind push to the turn-around spot, a spit of buildings and three large silver silos gleaming in the morning sun. Less helpful was the number of times he told me we were almost there. Note to self: A grain silo in Iowa appears to be one mile way from anywhere.

A local farmer took one look at my gloves and dug out a pair of camouflaged hunter's Gore-Tex models from the back of his truck.

"What's with the index fingers?" I asked. While still insulated, this digit cover was thin and offered more mobility.

"That there is your trigger finger, son." He mimed a shotgun blast motion.

Of course the only animals not holed up inside burrows and hidey-holes were us, so a bit of hunting was out of the question unless someone turned the ride into Richard Connell's "The Most Dangerous Game."

Another bit of advice: Never wear metal-rimmed eyeglasses in arctic conditions. At least they kept my eyes from freezing shut, but visibility was reduced to periscope level. Which was all for the best because I missed the Iowa-girls-gone-wild lifting of shirts and opening of parkas. I'm a married man. Besides, the roadway, while plowed and salted, was dangerous enough without those kinds of distractions.

Every time I threatened to turn back, my posse from the paper and bike shop formed a protective pace line membrane around me. When I fell off the back I would make the sound of a llama during childbirth. This caused them to slow just enough so I could latch on again.

I tried busying myself with a swallow or two from a shop-provided water bottle. That futile act of kindness had frozen solid a few moments outside the town limits.

At the turnaround we were treated to "pork on a stick" and firehouse chili.

"It's been dead this year!" said the cute Tyson Foods volunteer as we purchased our charity meat Popsicles. "I don't think more than a hundred of you . . . you guys [read "crazy people"] braved it the entire way."

I noticed a woman trying to rub her feet back to life in the corner of the room. She was sobbing softly. Another rider was drinking lite beer served in a quart milk jug. Some of it had frozen to his beard.

But foolish behavior has its privileges. Upon my frosty return, like a survivor from the Shackleton Expedition hollering into my cell phone for directions to the church basement gym afterparty, I realized something: how good I had it back home. Reflecting upon my ordeal while gazing across a silent little community, all glistening and angel-wing white by snowfall, a weak winter afternoon sun and a cobalt-blue sky, I couldn't deny the ice age beauty of it all.

I'd found the below-zero, frozen field of dreams while pedaling through that frat-boy-on-a-double-dog-dare-sized nightmare ride . . . and it taught me to never, ever, bitch about bike fender season in the Northwest again.

Chapter 13

AMERICAN PICKERS

There's nothing like finding gold, within the rocks hard and cold
I'm so surprised to find more, always surprised to find more.
—Avett Brothers, "Kick Drum Heart"

The side of the road is a map of our lives, or at least postcards
from the edges of who we are by what we haul around with us. It's
where we leave our trash and some of our most prized possessions.

I know because I've found your stuff—pockets and panniers of
it—at one time or another from all corners of the globe. Things so
unwieldy I must bungee-cord them to the rack of my bike or jam
them in the trailer. Things so small it's only a trick of the light and
the geometry of chance that reveals their presence.

I believe the bicycle makes modern-day Magellans out of its riders, moving at the perfect tempo and setting the exact vantage point
to bird-dog lockets, fedoras, drumsticks, and intimate diaries: docu-
menting marriages in crisis, long-running battles to keep off those
last fifteen pounds, and the nameless musings of a literary skate punk
explaining, with thesis clarity, why he thinks the band Bad Religion
stomps Led Zeppelin into the pavement—he's wrong, of course,
but I appreciate his rage and enthusiasm.

Bike gloves, bowling balls, engagement rings, compilation CDs, swimmer's ear medicine, and screen-damaged iPods.

Call me, leave a full description at the beep, and you might, and I say might, get your stuff back. Odds are against you, though. As that cockeyed *Saturday Night Live* philosopher Jack Handey once mused, "If you drop your car keys into a boiling river of lava, just let 'em go, 'cause baby, they're gone."

Which reminds me, I've got enough car keys to start a used lot, if I could only locate the cars.

It's not that I want your child's powder-blue unicorn named, oddly enough, Blackie. Believe me, it's a part-time job just trying to give away much of the crap that amasses in my own life. It's that I've already listed these on Craigslist and other spots you might go to find them, with few takers. But you never know. Around here, Goodwill runs happen on weekends.

Here's the thing. Most of that stuff you never needed to begin with; none of us do. Except for the occasional item soaked in memories, most of this gear just weighs you down. Those seemingly utilitarian or overtly frivolous things that came from someone once important to you, talismans bearing witness to our days: It's hard to let these go. I don't know which are which so eventually I might give a piece of your life away that you really wanted back. My bad.

Why pick these things up to begin with?

Beats me. Too many viewings of *The Treasure of the Sierra Madre*? Indiana Jones and the Temple of the Thriftstore? A good story to tell later? The thrill of the find? That self-important feeling you get when you return something of meaning to another person? Or because I can always use an almost new pair of cycling gloves once I've run them through the wash half a dozen times. (No amount of cleansing is too much when we're talking about another's bike gloves. Go take a whiff of your own athletic gear, if you don't believe me.)

And for every item I do pick up, there are a dozen more I spot, duly note, and leave for another treasure hunter.

There's even a technical name for roadside flotsam and jetsam: mongo. I know, it sounds like the nickname for that troubled transfer student who spend most of fourth-grade PE quietly rubbing up against the climbing rope, but there's a whole subculture built around the finders-keepers way of life: websites, books, claw tools to make dumpster diving easier. I'm a card-carrying member who didn't know it. Actually, I'm an unclassified offshoot because I only mongo in transit. Only collect while I'm in the saddle.

I'm a Mongo Biker.

Which makes me sound more hip and stylish than the reality of pedaling uphill connected to my kid's trailer, sans child but loaded with a perfectly usable, nearly empty beer keg, three Day-Glo pool floaties, and a license plate from 1947. When we look at it in that context, there's a good chance I'm a only a few pedal strokes away from becoming Harrison Ford's brilliantly deranged dad in *The Mosquito Coast*. There's a better chance you've mistaken me for homeless when, in fact, I believe myself to be a well-adjusted member of the community who chooses when I want to sleep out of doors. Hmm.

Enough self-examination, let's have a look at some of my mongo collection . . . and choice items gathered by others in the mongo cycling brotherhood. Oh yes, I'm not alone. There's an army of us, snatching stuff from obscurity, weather damage, and destruction. And very often, snatching items without dismounting or breaking stride.

Kevin was quite proud of a plaid blazer (like something a 1950s lounge singer would wear) found while riding outside of Palm Springs . . . he wore it for a while, but claimed it wasn't aerodynamic enough. (Plus, there was sand in the pockets.)

My take? Kevin didn't find his inner Sammy Davis in time to work the blazer into his act of daily living. Which is a shame, because we need more cyclists sporting lounge wear.

One mongo pedal pusher told of a baby stroller and connected baby car seat spotted in a ditch. Upon somewhat tense inspection, no babies, but it was in very good condition. Because he was single he left it there. But it does recall the time I had to meet my wife and transfer kids from my bike to the car in the parenting Olympics we call our daily routine. With no room left for kids and car seat (I still had the baby in the Chariot trailer), I reached for the go-to tool, not duct tape but bungee cords, and lashed the seat to the trailer like a barnacle to the keel. I got some looks. Good times and solid training for cyclocross season.

And now for the lightning round:

Pants . . . that fit.

A steel guitar, in tune.

Oakley sunglasses, the transitional lens kind.

Cell phones—often with contacts, so they could be returned to their owners. We've met grateful owners at gas stations and hotel offices to make the handoffs.

North Face tent still in the box.

Piano with sheet music—no bench.

Sears could go out of business if people would just get their

Craftsman tools roadside:

Bundles of hacksaw blades. Best find ever. Haven't had a dull saw in fifteen years. A step drill, retail thirty-six dollars at Home Depot.

Sockets, screwdrivers, pliers, vise grips, wrenches, knives—one was thrown at the rider, who retrieved it. A find born from anger but still good for cutting pears.

Coleman multitool, Leatherman multitool and bar clamp.

And from the files marked True Life Dramas And We'll Never Know What Really Happened:

Mattress with a pair of jeans neatly folded up and a Bible placed on top.

Sharpshooter's medal (obviously missed its mark or he tired of always living the straightest line from point A to B).

Female elk head on Sauvie Island, Oregon. Probably dumped by poachers but perhaps a fierce battle with a black bear.

New Visa credit cards with the pictures on them. When the cyclist turned around to pick it up he noticed empty pistol casings on the ground close to it. He decided to just forget he saw anything and rode away.

And the most improbable find:

An artist/cyclist Bill carried the *tail* of a squirrel that his riding buddy Mark ran over. The wheel cut it off the squirrel (which ran away). Bill wanted the tail for some art project or hat, so into his pocket it went for the rest of the ride. Mark said a silent prayer and christened the animal Stubby because, unlike lizards, there are no records of squirrel tails growing back.

Mongo that sounds most like a song by the band Boston:

"I see a lot of stuff, but always end up finding peace of mind," one cyclist said. Greeting card deep, but true and in no small part because the bicycle takes you there and gives you the time and space to smell the roses, or search the bushes for good mongo. But it still sounds too much like a Boston tune that played continuously from 1978 until the summer of 1980 when, though I once loved the song, I joined local forces and raided the radio station. There were no survivors.

And the Most Important Piece of Mongo found in my own life . . . was me.

Beth stumbled upon me in a campground in Bryce Canyon, Utah. I'd tossed myself outside the bounds of society, using a bicycle to light out for the territories, hoping to find some clarity, exercise, and good stories along the way. I was a bit of human flotsam drifting away from the world in no particular direction.

Then Beth claimed me, lifted me out of myself, shined me up, healed the places that hurt, and decided I was worth keeping.

I became something of value by loving another tattered but pure soul with everything I had in me.

And as of right now, I have not been posted on Craigslist or dropped off at Goodwill.

Chapter 14

SAVING CHRISTMAS

The main reason Santa is so jolly is because he knows where all the bad girls live.

—George Carlin

Given the choice, never bike-camp behind a frat house during pledge week. In hindsight, leaving the lighthouse tour along Maine's coast was a mistake. I turned inland on a whim and things turned surreal. Dusk forced me to ground. I stashed my bicycle behind a stand of alders, pitched my low-profile tent, and drifted off.

In my dream Foreigner played with the knob torn off, funneled beer flowed, and pledges lost all inhibition with sorority sisters. What the law refers to as Class 3 felonies, good-time kids of privilege called "unwinding" and "blowing off steam."

The sounds of breaking glass and drunken stabs at Loverboy's "Working for the Weekend" brought me around. Even Loverboy shouldn't have attempted that song. My tent flooded with light, a prison yard during a jailbreak. When a Singing Santa broke into "Jingle Bells," I felt myself going down the rabbit hole.

There would be no leap for me until this party ran out of steam, or beer.

I poked my head up, a prairie dog testing the air. What I'd missed at dusk through dense fall foliage was crystal clear by 1 a.m. I'd camped in a ravine behind a frat house at the University of Maine.

Someone peed over the side of the porch. An empty beer can bounced off my tent. I like a good time, especially if that good time is gonna keep me up anyway. But if I'd emerged in polypropylene long johns, helmet hair, and a jarring biker's tan, materializing out of the New England darkness to offer up a few whoops, maybe belch the fraternity's Greek letters before reaching for a beer, I'd be looking at a good solid beating.

Trapped. I couldn't sleep or participate in a raucous game of strip twister on the patio. And Santa would not shut up. Apparently, someone else had qualms with the holiday keepsake on a song loop.

"Is this a sword?" someone asked, slurring his words.

"Sure is. Samurai! I bought it at the mall," answered a partygoer, rocking on a porch swing.

They mulled over staging a poor man's version of Bruce Lee's *Enter the Dragon*. Santa offered a enthusiastic rendition of "Deck the Halls" in his defense.

The Fat Man was a goner.

"Gimme that sword!"

Lots of laughter.

"Any last words, Santa?"

While his singing was torture to someone trapped in a tent, did Father Christmas really deserve execution? Then came the sound of a porch door swinging open.

"Hey, ass monkeys. Totally uncool. Shelly's mom lent us these decorations. You want to hack something? See those trees? They're all over New England."

Fraternity brother to the rescue. After some bitching, they fell in line. Thankfully, they were too drunk to brave the darkness, thus saving my squatter's camp being sliced to bits.

When St. Nick broke into a rendition of "I Saw Mommy Kissing Santa Claus," I too contemplated the merits of a sharp sword.

First light found me cold, tired, and surrounded by empty beer cans. I packed up. That should have been the end of it. But curiosity and all that . . .

The morning after was a Civil War battlefield with no survivors. A light fog blanketed everything. Utter silence that only alcohol consumed in quantity can produce.

I tiptoed up the steps. What was I hoping to find?

At least Santa's presence out of season was explained. Someone majoring in sloth had decorated for all the holidays at once: colorful lights, plastic pumpkins, a green leprechaun resting in the Nativity manger with Mary and Joseph kneeling over him, no doubt praying for answers as to why the son of God was a wild-eyed gnome swinging a pot of gold. It took me a moment to locate singing Nick. Someone had thrown the Twister mat over him. Only his black boots and the cuff of his red suit were exposed.

I removed the mat. He looked a bit rough. His pipe was hacked clean off, leaving only a small black nub. This gave him the appearance of a cigar-chewing crime boss or a rough-and-ready Yukon explorer. Also sliced was the top of his trademark cap, adding to the working-class look. Think Santa Brando in *On the Waterfront*. When

I pulled away the rest of the Twister tarp, he broke into song.

I was holding him up to locate an off switch when I heard the pack of dogs. Time to go. I have no good answer for why I brought Santa with me.

Working a bicycle up to speed with a two-foot plastic Santa stinking of beer balanced between one's knees—well, that's no picnic. I'd fidgeted on Santa's lap plenty of times as a child, but this was the first time he'd returned the favor.

We pulled up to an abandoned gas station. I set the fat man down beside a rusting Sunoco sign.

"Don't look at me like that, someone will be by for you. Maybe a nice family. Least I didn't leave you back on that porch."

Unfazed, Santa stared across the highway stoic. In my head I could hear him clear as day.

"Couldn't handle a bit of Christmas cheer on board, eh?" he said.

I'd been by myself too long. I pedaled away. He broke into a heartfelt version of "I'll Be Home for Christmas." I circled back.

"Look, they would have dressed you up in women's underwear and used you as an ashtray. You're better off this way."

He dismissed me with a couple of hip shakes and a Ho, Ho, Ho. That's when I realized Santa worked off a motion sensor. The technology was in its infancy back then, but still, this thing was state-of-the-art. He had three greetings and twenty-five songs. If Fatty detected movement, he'd toss out a hearty "Ho, Ho, Ho, Merry Christmas" or, for our neighbors to the south, "Feliz Navidad."

Someone had spent real coin on this keepsake.

Once you've saved a life you are responsible for it. Shit. I lashed Santa to the back rack with a bungee cord.

"If we're going to do this, I have some ground rules I'd like to go over."

Jolly little fucker broke 'em all.

He had speakers in the back of his head and his belly so I was getting the holiday spirit from all sides. When a good-sized truck blew by Santa detected motion and broke into song. Why not just turn him off when I wasn't in the mood? He had no off switch! No discernible latch, secret hatch, or hidden nest for batteries.

Strapped across the rack, Santa looked to be cloud gazing, working on his tan, or counting birds for the Audubon Society. Fine if we'd been pedaling across a desert, but every telephone line of starlings set him to song. Shifting my butt would cost me a "Feliz Navidad" or a few verses of "White Christmas."

By New Hampshire we'd worked some things out. For starters, I'd located his sensors. They were behind his eyes. Kinda creepy, but once you've made a few feet of singing plastic your traveling companion, the rest is of it is splitting hairs.

I moved him from the rack to one of the rear panniers. His top half sticking over the rim of the bag put me in mind of an old sailor scanning for land. If only he knew a few shanties. If I didn't want to hear from my fat friend, I'd blindfold him with a bandanna. Granted, this made him look like a condemned man awaiting the firing squad, but when I pulled the sash up to his forehead, he became a swashbuckler performing a giddy holiday medley.

I'd catch the wild-eyed bastard in my helmet mirror now and then, chewing the black nub of his cigar, grinning like a banshee. When the bandanna slipped to his neck and blew in the wind, I swore that a lost member of the Village People was riding shotgun.

"You call that pedaling?" he'd bark, all the while bugs and road debris clinging to his head. "My reindeer could teach you something about fight. There's no quit in those animals."

"Keep it up, Nicky. You'll be in the dark the rest of the day."

Santa didn't scare easy. I'll say this, though: My average speed improved. In my secret heart, I liked having a sidekick to egg me on, even if we drew stares . . . and our road show could have benefited from some Springsteen in the playlist. But let's face it, Santa was a conversation starter.

Who can resist dancing to a rowdy rendering of "Holly Jolly Christmas"? Not a pack of Hacky Sack–playing teens on the courthouse lawn in Hartford, I'll tell you that.

Roadside diner waitresses asked if Santa would like an order of cookies and milk, or a carrot for his reindeer. He was worth his weight at scoring me free desserts and veggies.

Another use: security. I'd assign Santa night patrol outside my tent when renegade camping. If anything breached the darkness he'd go off like a holiday theme alarm system.

I almost left him with my grandparents during a stopover. There were so many keepsakes around, what was one more? But they were getting on in years and needed to start downsizing. Besides, I think Santa's frat house scars and road grit frightened Nana a little.

In Virginia, we stopped for repairs. Brothers Cyclery was, in fact, owned by two bearded, aging brothers who could have been twins. I asked if this was the case.

"Don't you think we would have called it Twins Cyclery then?"

Reinforcing what I've always suspected: Many bike shop owners are socially handicapped curmudgeons who speak best through their Allen wrenches.

I made a throwaway comment about finding Santa's off switch. Next thing I knew one of the brothers had Nicky on the table performing a procedure below the waist with a screwdriver and a soldering gun. When the brother turned our jolly little man onto his side, there was eye contact.

Those motion-sensitive peepers looked deeply offended.

"Et tu, Bike Boy?"

But the fat man would not go gently into that good night. After the procedure, it was too quiet. My pace was slipping. Had I made a terrible mistake? At the North Carolina border, when I'd resigned myself to the atrocity I'd been complicit in, Nicky came back to life. No fanfare, he just started singing about dashing through the snow as we worked our way onto the Blue Ridge Parkway.

"You had me worried there, Fatty."

Only things were different. The procedure had neutered Father Christmas of his lower octave while giving him the hint of a speech impediment. A kid outside the Piggy Wiggly, moving cautiously around my plastic toy as it ran through its medley, put it best.

"Mister, your Santa is just scary!"

And that was before the dogfight.

On a back road north of Valdosta, Georgia, I broke one of my road rules: Never stop at a shade tree service station with more than three cars on blocks. The dogs rounded the corner just as I was finishing with the water hose. Fortunately, I'd remained on my bike. Turning the hose on the pack was the only way we got out of there alive. I could hear Santa taunting them with "It's the Most Wonderful

Time of the Year" the whole way.

I howled like a madman left too long in the sun. The dogs chomped at my heels. Santa sang through it all. Give 'em the business, Fat Man. Always leave 'em with a song!

Once clear, I could see that he'd taken one for the team. His left arm was gone. Ditto for 60 percent of his right ear.

"Wishing I'd left you back on that porch now, eh?"

But Santa's stare never faltered.

"And miss all this? Not on your life, Bike Boy!"

You can't fake that kind of can-do attitude.

In the years since, I've had many riding partners. And every single one of them . . . has been better company than a two-foot chunk of singing plastic.

But I'll say this: No one pulled me through a lonely little patch in my life with more flair, musicality, and thoughtful bullying than that fat bastard.

All along, I thought I was rescuing the Spirit of the Season. But it turns out the jolly little fat man, and the very best things he can still stand for, were saving me.

Chapter 15

OH WHEN
THE SAINTS ...

To play the trumpet you must train your lips a long time. When I was twelve or thirteen I was a good player, but I lost the skill and now play very badly. I do it every day even so. The reason is that I want to return to my childhood. For me, the trumpet is evidence of the sort of young man I was.

—Umberto Eco

Oh when the saints, go marching in, I wanna be in that number, as the guy bringing up the rear . . . on a bicycle. Riding no-hands, pedaling through those ornate gates, coaxing soulful sounds out of my trumpet, Technicolor notes pulled straight from my own book of jubilations.

You'll spot me easy enough, grinning ear-to-ear during the drum breaks, spinning my battered brass around like a Josey Wales six-shooter, and pumping the air with my free hand to that funky voodoo beat.

I took up the horn the first week of junior high, and it rarely left my side for the next decade. It was like coming home. At an age when precious little was on solid footing, it became my Gibraltar. That little rent-to-own instrument from Don Banks Music blew the doors wide to a safe, verdant space.

When I touched its cold metal to my pinched lips, there was a shift of the light inside my head. Just enough for me to see my way through the thickets to a fine little sugar shack; a ramshackle honky-tonk joint, shadowed by live oaks dripping with Spanish moss. Uneven planks, a dirt floor, and a tin roof. It was always just after sunset when I walked in. Baker, Gillespie, Davis, Armstrong, Alpert, James, all those cool-ass river cats were over by the bar, easy laughter, a haze of smoke, standing a few feet from a makeshift milk crate stage, taking requests. Anything I wanted to hear . . . or they felt like playing. While they got high between the notes, I chewed up their riffs and swallowed those melodies whole.

It was 1978 in south Florida. Of course my secret garden would be a backwoods speakeasy full of the baddest Black, Cuban, and Mexican horn section of the millennium. I'd put on headphones in my parent's darkened study, plunk down the needle on record after record, and let the warm bossy brass act as siren songs, leading me into the deep woods.

When I came out the other end I appeared relatively unscathed by my teen years. Was I still a wet hot mess of feathered blond hair, jutting Adam's apple, and improbably patterned terry-cloth shirts throughout the experience?

Believe it.

But making music, badly at first, then with a certain roughneck flair, kept me from making a complete mockery of the decade.

Our band teacher, Mr. Crosby, was a rather strange, exotic bird.

Aside from actually resembling a bird—tall, thin, with a pinched face, pointy nose, and owl glasses—he had this hunch across the length of his back and a convertible European sports car that no longer went in reverse. Some mornings I'd see him circling the block, cruising for a slot to come available that was long enough to ease in nose-first. Blood, Sweat and Tears or Zeppelin blasting from the car stereo. Other times it was the local jazz or big-band stations. On those days he reminded me of a turkey vulture, circling and circling. He never went for the stealth arrival.

At recess, he was just as conspicuous. Mr. Crosby, or Crosby as we were told to address him, would knock out twenty behind-the-neck pull-ups. The bars were right there in the middle of the action. His hunch made it nearly impossible to do regular ones. Students would stop a four-square game or look up from a good book to witness this curiosity. The stares did nothing to break his routine until it became everyone's routine; mundane, a forgotten part of the landscape. In fact, he carried himself in all situations as if a bulky hunch was no big deal . . . so it wasn't. In addition to teaching me how to play the trumpet, he gave all of us this nugget at no extra charge: Pull up your collar, no matter how misshapen you might be, and play your own game. If he only knew how far that's gotten me . . .

And he gave me something else: my first gig.

I'd only been playing for a semester, but was a quick study and really got off on making music. The transistor radio tuned to Top 40 had been a staple under my pillow most nights since I was three years old, but to actually create music myself, even if it was Rocky's training montage theme song or *Hawaii Five-0*, turned me into a different person. A person I thought I could get behind.

That spring, Crosby pulled me aside during lunch—he took it each day lone-wolf-style in the band room—looked me straight and hard in the eye, and let go of a long sigh before he spoke. I braced against bad news and his coffee breath. Had the ninth-grade percussion section perished in a bus crash coming back from regionals? Had they hospitalized people from the woodwind section for heatstroke? Everyone knew wearing those wool uniforms in Florida during the Ybor City Night Parade was courting disaster. It was like donning a suit of armor in the tropics.

"Kurmaskie. You will report to the main office five minutes before the start and close of every school day." He handed me a pamphlet of sheet music titled *US Army Bugle Calls*. "Learn 'To the Colors' and 'Retreat.' You'll stand at the doorway exactly three marble squares back from the entrance into the courtyard. The acoustics there are perfect. Resonates through all three floors of the building without man-made amplification. Mark Howl is moving on to high school at the end of the semester and we can't have a break in the tradition." He gave me another long, studied look. He had not released the bugle calls pamphlet from his grip yet.

"This is an honor I'm offering you, so I need you to take it serious."

I tried to pull myself taller in the folding metal band chair. I thought about saluting him, but it seemed the wrong gesture to a man working through a homemade PB&J off butcher paper and drinking government-packaged chocolate milk through a straw.

Patsy Cline's "Crazy" played softly on a radio in his office.

"Should we do some push-ups to seal the deal?" I asked. This was a ridiculous thing to say, but his stare had me so nervous I could only think about how contented he looked doing his recess pull-ups.

Crosby released the pamphlet into my possession, sucked the last of the chocolate milk, and showed teeth when he smiled. "It's okay if you only manage fifteen, but I'm going to knock out the standard twenty-five."

I did all twenty-five and arrived a full ten minutes early the following Monday morning. Standing at attention with my horn behind my back, I waited for the bell to ring so I could debut "Call to Colors." I'd practiced it so many times that weekend, my father joked during Sunday dinner that he was back in the Coast Guard.

Howl wandered in with ten seconds to spare, brought his horn up to his lips, pulled it back again, and whispered, "At ease, Gaylord. Follow my lead and don't you dare fuck it up by playing louder than me."

Howl was all right as far as bullies went. He was built like a brick house. I made the mistake of pointing out the irony of this while he was wearing his Commodores BRICK HOUSE T-shirt. It hurt to lift my shoulder that week but you get two for flinching. At one point I covered for him with the principal, offering a plausible story for why he wasn't by my side playing his horn. The truth had him in the stairwell making out with the new transfer student who didn't know he was a douchebag yet. I had him assisting the safe load-out of the handicapped kids coming back from a field trip.

"Quick thinking with that story, Chief."

For the rest of the year he treated me like his favorite pet. I still got hit sometimes, but he'd also share candy, try unsuccessfully to get girls to flash their boobs by saying I'd never seen one in the wild (true), and stopped calling me Gaylord. The full measure of his acceptance was that when he was with his peers, he acknowledged my existence with mildly racist and derogatory nicknames, but always toned in a playful voice. And when he threw debris at me while I was pedaling to or from school, it wasn't liquids or gum . . . and he'd given the word to his friends . . . never at the head.

On the last day of school, it felt like inheriting a vast estate. Sam Queirolo would be my wingman next year. He'd been joining us at the marble squares during the final week of classes, to get the hang of it.

"Okay, buttholes, remember . . ." Howl tapped my chest with the front of his horn. "Play 'Hit the Road Jack' or I will be hitting your faces."

So many things ran through my head in those few seconds. My unspoken pledge with Crosby, sealed with push-ups, confirming my seriousness to the vocation. Howl's fist the size of a saucepan. Sam looking to me for what to do. This was not what he'd signed up for. Would Crosby call me a disgrace and keep me from doing the thing I loved, nearly craved, for the next two years? All for one glorious moment of rebellion? I settled on Crosby's school-yard pull-ups. His daily *Fuck You* to the universe.

"Let's do it, Sam. But Howl, we'll be playing louder than you . . . you piece-of-shit high schooler."

Howl could decide whether to bring up his fists or bring his trumpet up to his lips, but then he started laughing too hard to play. It didn't matter. Me and Sam rattled the building to its foundation with that tune. The cheers roaring back at us weren't really for us, but I soaked them in anyway.

Crosby pulled his sports car up to the stoplight. All I had to do was roll my bike back a little; without reverse, he wouldn't have been able to follow me. Instead, I held my ground.

"Hey, Kurmaskie!"

I looked over.

"Howl never could take anything serious!" Crosby knew the tone and timber of every student's instrument under his tutelage, and how many instruments were playing at any given moment during our band rehearsals. Fashion, food, cars, these were afterthoughts for Crosby, but music was his life. And here he was giving me an obvious pass, my own *Fuck You* to a cold universe, a get-out-of-jail-free card.

His trombone case was sticking out from the little car's rumble seat. He had signed off our last band class of the year by telling his students that he played in an American Brass Quintet, hired to roam the local malls and perform throughout the summer.

Most of my peers interpreted this as fair warning. I thought I might just check them out.

"Have a great summer, Mr. Crosby."

Chapter 16

TO YOUR SCATTERED BODIES GO

One ought, every day, to hear a song, read a fine poem, and, if possible, speak a few reasonable words.

—Johann Wolfgang von Goethe

It doesn't matter what I'm doing, when the first chords of any Led Zeppelin song kick in, I'm pulled back thirty-five years—a shop-vac sucking me through a wormhole.

We've parked the tandem against a cottonwood tree. There's a festival of some sort happening in Tom McCall Waterfront Park It's being soundtracked with *Zeppelin IV*.

Someone has impeccable taste.

As sailboats zip across the Willamette River, I explain to Quinn, my oldest son and stroker for the day, that in the 1970s, when "Stairway to Heaven" came on the radio, no matter where or what or who—it could be getting ready for a dance, or late for school, or trying to pack all that polyester and Farrah hair into the backseat of a Camaro at the end of some after-school practice, everyone needing to get home, it didn't matter—if the first chords of "Stairway" came on, you stopped what you were doing for seven minutes and forty-eight seconds.

Gonna get in trouble for being late? Well fuck it, that's "Stairway" on the radio so sit your ass down, do not look for your keys or the exit, or say another word about all the shit you have to do. Just chill and let Zep take you away from this bullshit reality for a spell.

God help anyone who tried to turn it off after the first chord or two. The entire population, from disco queens to speed metal freaks to Karen Carpenter fans, were experts when it came to picking out "Stairway" from a dial of songs up and down the bandwidth.

"Hey, hey, hey . . ." was all anyone had to say and the offending party would be properly chastened, nod in agreement, and turn that rock-'n'-roll ballad up to eleven as penance. Any snacks or drinks they'd been holding on to got dished out and passed around for their colossal lapse in judgment.

In my circle this became known as the Zeppelin Protocol.

We're on a rare father–teenage son Sunday bike ride. Rare as a white rhino these days. All those miles and unbroken months with him as my copilot; nine thousand miles by bike across the USA and Canada. I convinced myself he'd be my little boy, seeing the world over my shoulder forever. Like my own mortal enterprise, knowing it would end but never believing it. The sting was excruciating the first time he turned down a chance to ride together. It got easier over time, but I never stopped asking.

What teenager wants to do the bicycle-built-for-two routine? That's why I tried to play it cool when he stunned me with his own invitation. I felt like a schoolgirl and knew I was putting more signif-icance to it than warranted . . . but it could be our last ride . . .

Zeppelin's "The Levee Breaks" comes on. Quinn nods, "This shit was in *True Detective*. It's really good."

I smile. "Yeah, but before it rocked hard on *True Detective*, it sound-tracked my teenage existence."

I get a faraway look in my eyes. "I remember hanging out after a church car wash at St. John's Episcopal when this Gran Torino fish-tails into the parking lot. I don't recognize the driver, but Kip's in the passenger seat. He was this kid from my sister's class two grades ahead. He wore tinted aviator glasses and flicked a lighter everywhere he went. I'm in a terry-cloth shirt sweating it out in the late-afternoon Sunday heat. Kip says, 'Get in, we'll drop you.'"

Understand that I've just accepted a ride in a Gran Torino when my bicycle is in perfect working condition, locked in the church's bike cage not twenty-five yards away, basically because Kip scares the hell out of me. He carried around fire and flaunted it no less . . . and no adult had taken it away yet.

One constant in my life, besides the bike, is that when I leave the saddle of my bicycle for the confines of a car, it rarely ends well.

Once inside, the backseat felt like another cage. They passed around a joint and said they needed to make a couple of stops, but I'd get home eventually . . . laughter was crushed under the first blues chords, those rumbling drums and that massive wailing harmonica. Kip and his Gran Torino hooligans found a flat expanse of grassy median along the Bayshore and decided this demanded they do donuts. It's 4 p.m. on a Sunday, car filled with smoke, spinning wildly in circles, plastered against the glass like I'm on an outlaw carnival ride, the sounds of Zeppelin rattling my ears, those drums beating back space and time, and Kip casually tosses a book back at me.

"You gotta read this, man. It'll blow your mind." I'm holding tight to whatever I can grip and praying, but I do love a good book. If I'm gonna die I might as well go out knowing the title. I fight the g-forces and astronaut my head down far enough to read the title: *To Your Scattered Bodies Go*, by Philip José Farmer. It's the first book in the Riverworld series. And while nothing is *Lord of the Rings* and we might be looking at scattered bodies all over this boulevard shortly, I do like the title.

Somehow we survive all that power sliding and come to a stop in a 7-Eleven parking lot. I realize I'm alive and safe thanks to "Stairway to Heaven," which subdued the driver's stunt car intentions. People pile out and sit on the curb, blasting the song.

I ponder how anyone could keep such a high-profile sports car, drugs in the open, tearing donuts on a median strip, and not be in jail. It comes to me that this guy has been driving for all of six months. Time hasn't caught up with him yet. I don't want to be there when it does. Munchies in hand, they pile in, but I've already made my escape . . . with the book. When Kip kicks the door wide and folds the seat for me to get back in, I wave him off.

I'm miles from my house and an equal distance from my bike, but I refuse the ride.

"It's cool." I say. "I need the air."

He flicks his lighter a few times, like he's considering burning it all down, then his stare turns into a smile.

"Dig it," he says before they peel off into a summer of high-octane adventures, jail time, or death.

Zeppelin ringing in my ears, I thumb the first page of the book open for the long walk back. By the end of the trek my heart is pounding for new reasons and by the end of the summer I've reread it three times and launched an all-out search for the rest for the series.

"So something good did come out of Kip's death-wish ride," Quinn says.

I nod as we go to load ourselves onto the tandem. The memory of those g-forces, the sound of a flicking lighter, flying mud, pot smoke, and fear in my throat pinned to the back of a Gran Torino still makes me shiver. "You could argue Kip did me a favor offering me a ride that day, but it's my experience that libraries and bookstores are a safer route to quality literature."

Quinn likes this. He says, "You know, Dad. Most of your stories don't suck."

High praise.

I look back to see if my stoker is ready to roll, but Quinn's dismounting.

"Zeppelin Protocol," he says. It's then I realize that "Stairway" has come up in the rotation.

We lean the tandem against the cottonwood again. This time we sit at the base of its wide trunk. He produces some candy he's been holding out on me. It's not my favorite but I take it anyway. I put my hand on his shoulder and he doesn't shrug it away. There's no holding back the passage of time. I'm its hostage as much as anyone, but for the next seven minutes and forty-eight seconds we manage to slip its bounds and leave the bullshit of reality behind.

And as we wind on down the road
Our shadows taller than our soul . . .

Chapter 17

THE WONDER OF BOYS ... ON BIKES

Much of parenting is improv, controlled chaos, and snatches of unbridled joy once one learns to sit and savor in the eye of the storm.

When your transportation is a bicycle rather than a minivan, there is no eye, just unrelenting, unending storm. The only reasonable answer then is to become the storm.

Sawyer's show-and-tell letter for the day is *H*. I learn this just as we pedal off to school. Now we're standing in the living room again, still wearing our helmets and rain gear.

"How about a helicopter?" I hold up a cheap toy prize won at the arcade. One of its blades is broken.

"What about a hug?" Beth suggests.

Sawyer looks at her with a mix of scorn and pity.

"Hat?" I toss out there. Literally, I toss the hatbox onto the living room floor.

He touches one of three hats we are trying to pass off as Indiana Jones, since the real Jones hat went missing a few weeks ago. He knows we're trying so he pets one of them. "Too furry."

"Hitchhiker. Why don't you pick up a hitchhiker and bring him to show-and-tell?" Beth is standing in the kitchen holding a massive bicycle-themed coffee cup. It's a replacement for her WORLD'S GREATEST MOM mug that Enzo's skater punk friend accidentally kicked onto the pavement and into a zillion pieces.

She misses that cup something awful, but she knows we're trying so she pretends the new one is wonderful.

"Okay, that crossed some sort of line, didn't it?" she says merrily. It's the coffee talking. I nod. "Also, Sawyer, we live too far from the interstate to find a first-rate hitcher before class starts."

We settle on helmet. The one currently on his head. It's covered in stickers, my favorite being the slice-of-bacon sticker. Usually the answers to life's show-and-tells are somewhere on you to begin with.

At a school drop-off one morning, we pedal upon two crows working over the fresh kill or accidental demise of a mouse in the middle of the road.

Sawyer yells, "Whoa . . ."

I break into the *Lion King* opening, followed by "Circle of life, my friend. The crows have to eat breakfast, too."

"Their mommies don't make them oatmeal?"

"No, with crows it's more a street buffet."

I'm approached by a dad in the checkout line at Sellwood Market who knows me by the bike I ride. He says, "Your oldest son? I see his clothes matching sometimes. He's a fucking Boy Scout. Mine is all odor and attitude . . . and attitude about the odor."

I tell him I'm not sure which one he's talking about because I have four sons. "If I had to guess, you're talking about the middle-ish older one."

We stand holding our six-packs in silence for an awkward moment. Then he whistle-whispers, "Four? Shit man. I had no idea."

Pedaling through an icy mist of rain this morning, Matteo rolling along behind on his own bike now like it's nothing but a thing. Maybe it was the hour or the mist but it reminded me of that long-ago morning in Pocatello, Idaho, when a blind old rancher gave me the name Metal Cowboy . . . and this other bit of advice I picked up recently.

Conditions are never perfect. "Someday" is a disease that will take your dreams to the grave with you.

Sawyer, just as we are embarking on our pedal over to his first day of preschool for the year, asks, "May I bring this, please? I put on my underwear and everything."

The *this* in question is a tree branch thick as a python and four feet long. He is attempting to jam it into the cargo bike pannier. He waves good-bye to his branch and notes that the neighbor's dog only barks when we are on foot, not on bicycle.

"I think we're a different creature when we're on the bike."

We always have been, SoySauce. And we always will be.

Matteo, after biking over together for opening day of a Pixar movie in 3-D: "Dad, if scientists can place false memories into the brains of mice, why no advancements on these 3-D glasses? All of 'em make the picture too dark and smudge up with popcorn grease before the previews are over." Regardless, he wears the glasses all the way home on the bike, looking like a deranged Stevie Wonder on two wheels.

"Matteo, you can't ride your bike in the house."

"You're wrong, Daddy, I'm doing it right now!" At least he knows the difference between *can't* and *don't*.

Sawyer, waiting on the porch while I have a moment in the bathroom ten yards away. I hear him telling everyone passing by:

"My daddy was in Vegas, now he's in the bathroom."

They say your hearing is the first thing to go. They're wrong. It's your dignity . . . slips free and floats out of reach with each act of parenthood . . . like a beautiful red helium balloon. And it helps if someone breaks this news to you by singing it in German.

As I'm getting the little boys into helmets and onto the cargo bike Beth calls out, "Should the older boys' room smell like wet wood chips in a hamster cage?"

"If they owned hamsters. Look, I thought you weren't to go down there anymore unless there was a perceived or legitimate medical emergency."

We stand in the morning light pondering the collective and individual choices that have led us to this moment. There are no answers, only the remains of the day . . . and the faint smell of wet wood chips.

Sawyer's smile, two games of Trouble, and some cold egg scraps left for me by accident have buoyed my spirits. I just need any effort out of my teenagers in the morning to feel like they have a little skin in the game.

Barring that, I have decided to take from Zen teachings the Koan about two wolves that live inside each of us. One happy and light, the other desperate and dark. The one that survives is the one you feed.

"But master, my teenage sons keep giving the desperate one table scraps . . . by virtue of mindlessness and sloth and horrible table manners, mostly."

"Oh," the master says, "you have teenagers? Then set the wolves Koan aside and fill this cup with tea until it is near to overflowing."

"Is this to teach me that I, like this cup of tea, am full to over-flowing with misconceptions and projections of how my sons should act?"

The master smiles. "No, it's full of caffeine, you're gonna need that shit. Have a second cup after I'm gone."

RainBowie . . . As I pedal through the rain with the boys along the bluff—on our way home from school—the sun breaks out like a Renaissance painting. Channeling a submarine captain, I holler to my little crew to scan for rainbows.

"Jeeeezussss . . ." Matteo says. The angle of the road curves enough for me to look to the right. The boys are laughing in stunned wonder and jubilation.

"Crikey!" I yelp.

The fattest, most penetrating Technicolor rainbow in the known universe . . . and its starting point is right ahead of us . . . in the lagoon in Oaks Bottom Refuge, a bird sanctuary situated just beyond the bluff. It bends the length of the sky. An inglorious bastard of color and impermanence. On any day it would have taken my breath, but today I start to tear up.

"Boys, we're gonna call it a RainBowie, and let me tell you why."

I host a brief David Bowie workshop under the arc of his stardust salute. The man who fell to earth for a time had left us that very day.

We stand in silence a bit longer.

"From now on, I'd like to call them all RainBowies," Matteo offers.

Mouths of babes . . .

The ride took longer than usual, but it was worth it since later my sons begged me to keep playing Bowie songs through round after round of living room foosball.

I'd like to think we keep coming back to earth in different permutations until we get it right. Then we get to come back once more . . . as David Bowie, only this time we get to remember everything that's come before . . . would account for that twinkle in his eye . . . and everything else he left us.

Chapter 18

BIKES, BLUEBERRIES, BLUE SKIES... AND DEATH THREATS

The Papa Wheelies—that's our dads cargo bicycle gang—met up along Portland's Springwater Corridor near the Willamette River for a summer afternoon of wholesome rolling fun.

We pedaled our troop of a dozen cargo bikes, bakfiets, tandems, Trail-a-Bikes, and about two dozen adults and children along a dedicated path the ten miles to Armstrong's Berry Farm. Several members of today's gang are honorary—not papas but mamas, because we're casual and inclusive like that . . .

After much merriment and slight uphill effort through a bit of traffic on the only mile of the journey that put us on a road shared with cars, we made the final push to the farm, arriving safely in staggered waves of a minute or two.

Josh (Baby Wheelie, at twenty-six years young) and myself are the first to arrive at the barn door. We all have nicknames; I'm referred to as Papa Bear (mostly by me and sometimes Andy) or mocked as Grandpa Wheelie since I'm the oldest of this group at forty-eight.

But seeing as I have no grandchildren it's playfully cruel and completely irrelevant since I often lead with two children in tow . . . so *Suck it* is my standard response, delivered with a devilish grin of course.

We find ourselves ungreeted by an elderly farm couple.

Josh offers up smiles and I toss out an "Afternoon." Crickets . . . then a grunt of a hello. Josh, undaunted, lets them know we have a pack of cyclists not far behind, bringing them a heap of business. I step into the barn and lean against a table to chat with the old man. I take a New Mexico rancher approach, nod, wait, wait a bit longer before speaking.

"We biked over here from Sellwood."

He squints. I tell him that's back in Portland, next to the river.

"You know they have this thing called a car now."

I chuckle. "And I own one, but try to let cobwebs build on it. Biking is so much more fun, helps us stay young, it's easier on the planet . . ."

He grunts, folds up his newspaper, and points up to the rafters. Three vintage bikes hanging up there covered in cobwebs—reminders of missed opportunities. Nothing sadder than bikes eight feet off the ground forever.

That's when the bulk of the Papa Wheelies roll through the gate and start disembarking out by rows of blueberries. There's laughter, conversation, a comfortable rolling-carnival-type vibe.

"And here comes the rest of your profit center for today." I gesture at the gang.

That's when the elderly woman, who has been preparing weighed containers for us to use, turns to me and says,

"We hate bike riders."

The old man chimes in. "They run stop signs and get in the way. I don't think you should be allowed on the road."

I start in about how there are good and bad road users in every transportation mode.

"You're just in my way," he adds before I've even completed my thoughts.

I try to stay reasoned and calm, but as I start to get angry, something happens . . . I hold back a flood of fury, replacing it with pity. I just feel bad for these two aging people with so much unnecessary bitterness in their hearts. I do the unthinkable for Joe Kurmaskie of five years ago . . . I walk away.

I head over to the gang. Deciding if we should still pick there or not, when I catch the woman saying something to Josh. He's been making our case, telling her that this group are all dads and moms, and that we try to follow the rules of the road and be examples of safety for our children.

She cuts him off with, "You bikers make me so angry, you slow me down when I need to get into town. I'd like to run all of you over . . . and your kids."

Josh, pale and gut-punched, marches over to us. I'm already taking blueberries out of some of the kids' hands.

I say, "Looks like we're not gonna play Sun City!" (an Apartheid music industry reference that I'm not sure the other Papa Wheelies get).

Josh and I relay to the gang what just happened. Everyone looking back at the old folks who stand there like statues, hardhearted, unwavering. We pedal hundred of dollars of blueberry money back out of their gate.

We regroup at the front of their entrance—pose ourselves for a thumbs-down photo of their sign, then look up where another farm might be. Turns out Josh thinks he remembers another one very close. He pedals up the hill all of *one* block to find Powder Blue Berry Farms. Like the scene in *O Brother, Where Art Thou?* when they hear the sound of singing from beautiful, winsome young sirens down by the river, we roll up to a pack of fresh-faced farm girls in tank tops and their cougar mom singing. Beyond them in the back acreage are a couple of strapping young guys getting onto farm equipment.

"Don't worry 'bout those two old crab apples. We love bikers. That couple has just a small patch and we don't see them as competition, but still they find out what price the berries are set at each week by the U-pick groups around town and then cut it by twenty-five cents, thinking they're stealing away business."

The next hour or two is spent in berry heaven. Kids running between the rows, faces covered blue. Farm animals for the kids look at. The gals gave us ice cream containers to pack home more berries for the freezer.

It was instant karma on the bitter harvest down the road. As we passed their sign once more, I felt the failure and missed connections—that their own human plants had grown so stiff and hollow. It's a mean world that forgets how little it takes to be kind, no matter by what transportation mode people use to arrive at your door.

We pedaled back to Andy's place, just off the trail, and made a blueberry cobbler in a Dutch oven. A summer sunset with the whole Papa Wheelie crew sitting around a campfire, enjoying good music and even better company.

Chapter 19

THE STALKER
OF SIESTA KEY

I've never fancied myself the stalker type. The only time I ever entertained the idea was after finishing a book by a favorite author. In high school, there was no bigger Stephen King fan than me. None. And don't let that jackass Danny Hampton from social studies class say otherwise. Did he know there was an unabridged edition of *The Stand*? No, he was working from a mass-market copy and talking out his ass. Still, on my first bicycle adventure from Maine to Florida I pedaled right by the King family residence in Bangor, Maine . . . without stopping.

My self-control never wavered. And it had nothing to do with the spooky iron-rod gate or gargoyle statues.

Of course critics of my not-a-stalker stance could point to the time I bamboozled mall security into jimmying this girl's car for me. We put a dozen roses in her front seat with a card taped to the steering wheel. It said something to the effect that what I felt for her could never be locked out. The kid in the security outfit kept giggling and asking if I surprised my wife like this often.

"All the time, champ. It's how to make a relationship last over the long haul."

Forget that we were about the same age, I was on a bicycle and not wearing a ring. Probably want to skip all that formal academy training and make him detective.

But back to the breaking, entering, stalking, and wooing. In my defense, well, there is no defense for creepy shit like that. We'd only had lunch a few times at the food court. Technically, more a case of talking to each other since we happened to be there at the same time.

But understand this, it was a very bleak period for me. And she purred on about how I looked kinda hot in the Banana Republic shirt she'd sold me. Come to find out that all male customers were told by female employees that they looked hot in any item they showed the slightest interest in. It's a significant part of the Republic's staff training.

If I *were* to stage a plausible defense, it would go like this . . . I was crazy from the Florida heat of working twelve-hour shifts at the mouth of a commercial oven, burning my fingers serving wood-fired pizza slices at the front end of a mall restaurant. Every moment inside the mall I was bombarded with Christmas Muzac. The restaurant was run by assholes who pretended they were in the mafia, but were really just assholes and not even Italian. Two from Brazil, one Spaniard; all assholes.

Also, my roommates, who had all flown back to Buffalo together for the break, borrowed my car to get to the airport and ten days later I still couldn't find it . . . and the airport parking meter was running. I pedaled up and down six levels of parking garage until I wanted to kick the bike against a curb and cry in frustration. Oh, and I'd just buried Travis Otis McGee, my cat, named after author John D. MacDonald's longest-running character.

I should have gone back to my empty apartment and listened to Tom Petty's *Hard Promises* again. Instead, I bought those roses and turned a Hallmark card into something just this side of a ransom note. The fallout included a visit by a posse of her mean girlfriends. They ordered slices and ordered me to keep my distance from their girl, and the Banana Republic in general. Unless I wanted to experience death by angora sweater suffocation. Nothing as treacherous as mall girls on a mission, though the one wearing the actual angora winked, circling back later to tell me how I could stalk her with roses anytime. It was all very confusing for me.

After that I didn't go to the mall, any mall, for about seven years. This was not by court order, though who would blame her? I just didn't like what I became inside those climate-controlled environments. A confused, petty, rancid little creature packed to the gills with Cinnabons and Orange Juliuses, staring into a shallow wishing pool full of small change and cheap tile.

So you'd think with that track record, I'd have looked hard in the mirror the day I decided to drop in on acclaimed writer John D. Mac-Donald. I discovered, by accident, that one of my favorite authors happened to live on Siesta Key, not too far from, but worlds away from, my off-campus apartment.

I place a copy of *The Lonely Silver Rain* on the bookstore counter.

"Loved this one," the woman behind the register says. "He's a bit of a chauvinist, but that's on account of the parlance of that time, and the time he came of age as a writer."

I nod. "I've read this one twice, but there are parts I want to circle back through and highlight."

She understands. She's holding a copy of Joy Williams's *Breaking and Entering* that looks to be on its fourth or fifth run-through. I see some notes in the margins. We talk about Williams's subtle hand at foreshadowing. We've made a connection.

"You know MacDonald lives right on Siesta Key." She's letting me into the circle.

I did not know this. The ghost of my Stephen King drive-by weighs heavy on my mind. If I could get a brief sit-down with Mac-Donald, writer-to-writer, man-to-man, a bottle of whiskey and two shot glasses, he might get me sorted out proper.

Everything had changed since the King sortie. I was an almost published novelist now. My first book sold to the University of Michigan. At twenty-three, I was to take the literary world by storm. Editors were saying such flattering things about my prose. A two-inch mention appeared in *Publishers Weekly*. Then the chairman of the department championing the project died.

Advice to aspiring writers: The guy who believes in your project and has walked it through the university press system should not be eighty-three years young with a bum ticker. Shop around. You might want your first agent to be a teenager. If you're still on your first draft, maybe they haven't been born yet. I received a kill fee that allowed me to bike across Australia and New Zealand, and gave me a lifetime of experiences. But the book went into a drawer at my parents' place and that literary fire in my belly, all that momentum, went somewhere else.

I needed an honest-to-goodness kick-in-the-ass pep talk from a master with fifty books under his belt, including a beloved Florida noir series featuring a tortured protagonist who salvages lives while navigating through cautionary tales of environmental destruction and spiritual exhaustion.

I come to find out he's getting up from his afternoon nap a few miles down the road?

There's nothing to consider. We need to meet.

This is what happens when a creative type is given a living wage to wander around bookstores on a Tuesday. He'll find additional ways to fill his time. I go back to the stacks, scoop up half a dozen other titles by MacDonald, have the clerk rough me out a map to his place, and begin pedaling my bike over to Siesta Key.

An actual plan might have been helpful. He doesn't so much live on Siesta Key as own a good chunk of it. I find a spot in the shade outside the security gate and ponder my options. I could hire a boat to pilot me around to the beach-access side of his place—a Normandy-type invasion. Only that would leave all these books I was hoping to have John sign soaking wet or back on the boat.

Sweating under a magnolia tree, listening to crickets in the middle of the afternoon, I see this latest flight of fancy for what it is. I'm gonna get shot or arrested or . . .

A pair of trucks hauling gardening equipment pull to the gate. I scoop up my bike and without hesitation pedal alongside the vehicles as they pass through. Once beyond the protection of the gardeners' trucks, my new plan loses its momentum. I expect to be clotheslined by security hiding in the palmetto bushes by now. So sure in fact that I ride clenching every muscle, awaiting impact. I would be taken to a safe room where my skills of conversation would convince everyone that John and I need to meet. When that doesn't happen I coast around the expansive grounds, unsure of my next move. I resemble one of those devil-may-care characters in a British novel. Wealth, privilege, and too much free time find him pedaling around the gardens thinking up the next witty thing to say at dinner. I lap the estate twice before meandering to a stop at the front entrance.

I might as well give it a shot.

I lean the bicycle against a massive column. The main building is southern Gothic plantation architecture. My backpack is heavy with mass-market tenth and eleventh editions, and used at that so Mr. MacDonald didn't see a dime from my recent purchases. I wait at the door. The surveillance cameras must be well hidden. I wait some more. When security still doesn't swarm, I knock. A Hispanic woman answers. I stammer something about my writing credentials and needing to meet with the author of *Condominium*, which incidentally they made into a horrific miniseries, completely missing all the ecological messages in favor of soap-opera dialogue and special effects. She stands with her arms crossed.

When I've talked myself out, she whistles.

I mistake this for admiration, not a call for backup. I believe I've persevered, stormed the castle in a novel, nonthreatening way and will now be granted audience with one of my literary idols.

A Samoan the size of a grizzly bear fills the doorway. I brace for the beat-down.

"He's not here." I notice a big bowl of cereal the Samoan is cradling. He studies me while steadily spooning, what is that, Special K? into his cave-like mouth.

"Is this the part where you rough me up?" Thinking I sound just like one of the characters in a MacDonald novel.

The Samoan shakes his head, grins. "Why? You want me to?"

As I see myself off the grounds, one of the gardeners waves.

"I thought you just wanted to have a look at the place." Back at the bookstore, now. The clerk is shaking her head. I can see she's pissed. "Like those maps of the star tours out in LA. You don't go in!"

What did she imagine I wanted with all the titles of his books I'd already read? I share my University of Michigan failed publishing saga to demonstrate my special purpose here. I'm not just a fan, but a peer. These are credentials that place me outside the stalker category.

She recoils. "If you want to hassle him for writing advice, I won't be party to that."

And I thought we'd bonded over our mutual admiration for the man and a respect for Joy Williams. I try one more thing.

"Have you ever met him?" Fans love to talk about their own encounters. She hesitates. Maybe an aspiring writer herself who thinks there's too many of us already.

The old guy behind us stocking biographies chimes in. "We've all met him." The clerk shoots this guy daggers, but he laughs it off, enjoying himself. "He's a regular. Most days he's down at the sandwich shop having Cuban coffee and garbanzo bean soup about now."

I can't help but grin at the pissed-off clerk. Come on, Sister, share the wealth.

I haven't tasted a good Cuban sandwich in at least a day, so I slide into a booth that offers me a direct view of the famous author. Inconspicuous as possible, I peek at his jacket photo on the back of *The Executioners*. Twenty years of busted gravel road on his face, but it's him.

While working through two iced teas, I watch the man who put McGee through a lifetime of trouble protecting the powerless and standing up for the mangroves and the coral reefs. I rehearse different approaches in my head. It has to be just right or he won't treat me as a peer, won't see in me a younger version of himself asking his future what to do to achieve heartbreaking stories of aching beauty that illuminate the human condition.

I decide to hold off telling him I named my cat Travis Otis McGee, after his most famous protagonist. It served dual purposes because every time I called for my TOMcat it reminded me of Mac-Donald's books. The Otis part of the name I added, but then there was no mention of McGee's middle name in the twenty-book series, so I felt I could take a small liberty in completing the acronym. When I play this little anecdote in my head, I see a middle-aged lesbian with a subscription to *Feline Fun Monthly*. That's really not how I want to present myself to my literary idol.

John D. MacDonald coughs up some soup phlegm, spits it into a napkin, looks at it intently for a few moments, then returns to his bowl. It occurs to me that my idol has already told me everything I need to know on the pages of his books.

This up-close tête-à-tête could be the granddaddy of bad ideas. I am about to voluntarily destroy the mythology of an author I hold in high regard. I hear some quiet slurping in his direction.

The myth is already crumbling when my Cuban sandwich arrives. No getting away clean now. That's when I notice MacDonald staring at me staring at him. He has a world-weary look on his face because he knows what comes next. He's marked me as a fan.

He always was a good detective.

I reach into my pack and grip one of his books under the table; it doesn't matter which one, they were all brilliant. I remember disappearing into each and coming out the other end changed, right when I was in desperate need of changing. I give it one more squeeze and let it fall away. It's now or never. I do what must be done.

"What you looking at, old man?" I put it out there with more force than I intend.

MacDonald smiles, offers a little *I surrender* wave with his soup spoon, and goes back to his meal.

As I work through my sandwich I can barely taste it. I'm already thinking about stories, scenes, plot points, and characters.

Not his for once, my own.

All those people I haven't felt strong enough to take a crack at come rushing into my head.

I've just told a literary titan to go fuck himself, and it has set me free.

Someday, if I'm lucky, I'll be an old man choking down some soup with a helluva writing career in the rearview mirror, but there's a lot of road to cover, and I'm burning daylight.

On the way out, I place my copy of *The Lonely Silver Rain* on his table. I don't look back. There's nothing to see but a fading genius struggling through lunch and dealing with the privileges of participating in his own decay.

It's not the two shot glasses and a bottle of whiskey I'd imagined, but then it never was.

Chapter 20

BMW GUY

Scientific studies found men between the ages of 35 and 50 driving BMWs were most likely to be engaged in road-rage behaviors, aggressive driving and swearing, parking violations and excessive speeding.

—*The Guardian*

Time again to play "Homeless or Homeowner taking out the trash?" As much as I love and trust Enzo, my fourteen-year-old, and his work as our family trash and recycling coordinator, I believe in trust, but verification. So I'm standing in the first blush of a sunlit, beautiful morning, sorting out the glass from the blue bin into the yellow one, when a guy rolls by in his BMW and asks me if I have permission from the owner to hunt for cans. I tell him that, despite appearances, I am the owner. I'm thinking, *It's the sweatpants, isn't it?* His smile says, *Among other things . . . Many. Other. Things.* What I do say is, "I'm a writer." I offer this for reasons still vague to me. He doesn't seem to know what to do with that so I add, "But if you see any homeless guys rooting through my trash, let them. I have an open sort policy."

Round 2

I've taken on the role of informal caseworker for several of the homeless in our community. Folks in the hood stop me on the street sometimes, bring me bags of drop-off cans, sometimes clothes for the homeless. This is where a cargo bike comes in handy for me. As I leave preschool on my bike, another cargo dad mentions, "I put a big bag of cans out by your bike for David."

Flash forward ten minutes. I'm pedaling home with the cans all Grinch Who Stole Christmas–style, bungeed together with volleyballs and nets in the cargo holds and sticking out the back of the bike because I coach the elementary school team and today is the first practice of the winter season. Add to this a zipper failure on my red Mountain Hardware rain jacket mid-trip. The jacket is now riding up against my chin while the rest of its sides flap in the wind. And due to my wet moss-covered front yard and trying to carry too many flats of sale yogurt in the darkness the night before, my shoes are covered in mud. Also, what I like to think of as my going-out sweats have some mud on the knees—but I did prevent the yogurt from hitting the ground during the load-out so, despite appearances, all's right in my world. Finishing off my ensemble is a ski cap under my helmet and my prized thirty-year-old gloves that have the middle finger duct-taped. Pedaling along my merry way, I feel a car trolling me. I look back and, I shit you not, it's BMW Guy from the other morning with the recycling confusion.

He takes the whole thing in . . . the cans loaded up higher than my head, my muddy sweatpants, the jacket flapping in the wind . . . and just stares in slow-mo as he passes by. I see him looking at me in his rearview mirror. One of those *I got my eyes on you* hand gestures made famous by Robert De Niro in the film *Meet the Parents.* I consider giving him the middle finger, but it's duct-taped permanently in that position anyway. So I just wave and smile, mission accomplished. I laugh all the way home.

The Showcase Showdown Round

My bank's around the corner, literally. I could have (I have) wandered over in pajamas mistaken for plaid pants . . . and my just-pop-out-to-the-store slippers that look like men's low-cut Uggs if you squint and turn away in time. All the tellers and folks over there know me as the neighborhood writer guy with the bikeload of boys so if I spruce up to, say, my Chewbacca hoodie and come in alone, they ask me if I'm leaving the neighborhood the way someone might reference a spacewalk. But, just as we say to death, *Not today,* I speak another truth when I say I was dressed up, not Joe dressed up, but big-boy, real-world-acceptable attire. Button-down blue shirt, black wingtips, and a black wool/cashmere long coat. It's my father's Coast Guard coat and it's one of those things I'd want to save in a fire . . . Funeral? Wedding? A wonderful opportunity as Toyota's regional sales manager? I couldn't just want to look nice? Okay, I was headed downtown on consulting business, but the bank needed some signatures on refi for the other house in North Portland. I walk up and notice a familiar BMW partially blocking the crosswalk out front with its back end. Really? I so don't want to generalize but there is a whole section of the Internet devoted to photos of arrogant BMW parking jobs . . .

"They tell me you're our resident celebrity author!" He's all good-to-know-you excited. Perfectly reasonable that without a hefty bag of cans, my cargo bike, ski cap, sweats, three days of stubble, broken-zipper rain jacket, et cetera. I'm like that *Undercover Boss* show.

"More like the resident vagrant," I say. Having a bit of fun now. "Income properties." He's been listening in and nods over at my paperwork. "That's the way you do it." And because you don't need a BMW to be part of the go-go rat race, I smile back and say, "Money for nothing and your chicks for free." I don't know if he gets the reference. He's been grinning at the same pace the whole time, so it's hard to tell. Still no idea I'm the guy he gave the *I've got my eyes on you* De Niro gesture just days ago. I want to do something, a grand gesture à la *Dead Poets Society* or something. But I can't seem to work up too big a head of steam about this guy's power trip. It just seems silly. And let's face it, plenty of folks would see the choices I make and the way I spend my time as folly, so . . . Don't get me wrong, he's a proper ass, but mostly I'm just tired that we haven't collectively evolved beyond the shiny things and impressing one another and scraping it out like junkyard dogs while Rome burns to the fucking ground. Then I feel those thirty-year-old, beautifully ratty gloves in my pocket, the ones with the duct tape on the middle finger, and I perk up. I bring them out and set them on my lap like they are fine garments. After he gets a good look at them I slip them on and wait some more. And there it is. I can almost see the montage of my homeless-looking self colliding with my current persona in his mind's eye.

The word *nonplussed* is bull's-eye-accurate. I stand, hold up the gloved hand with the permanent middle finger, smile, and make for the door. Later, I thought that something forced and overly clever, like "If the glove fits, you can't acquit" would have iced the cake. But no, that involuntary, inadvertent middle finger while standing in my father's coat, inside the life I've chosen . . . priceless.

Intermission

Will you look at that? Guess who's been idling across the street from my house for the past fifteen, no twenty, ah for the love of twenty-five minutes, burning all those bargain-basement-priced fossil fuels!

BMW Guy must be closing a big deal in his mobile office. You got to stay warm and keep the soft-rock tunes cranking if you're gonna make that paper.

But BMW Guy, think about the chickens. You're choking out the free-range chickens that live just feet from your dual exhaust pipes.

Ah Jesus, he's wearing a Bluetooth jawbone phone. I come right up to the car and snap a photo of the whole thing. Like a UFO sighting, I want documentation for when people think I've let this unhealthy obsession with luxury car drivers get out of hand.

This thick brick thinks we've got extra planets hidden at Overstock.com. Passing the thirty-five-minute mark. That's it. Someone bring me my duct-tape gloves.

Cat's In The Cradle

Westmoreland Park, once the home to more goose poop than grass, has been transformed into one of these nature play meccas with the downed-tree-type structures and the boulders and areas to build forts, and a water feature where people leave buckets and toys for the community to share. Park usage is up something like 4 trillion percent.

Last week, during a weekday afternoon in the heart of the freak-ishly warm and bright weather we're enjoying, I pedaled Sawyer and Matteo over for some lightsaber battles in said park and general fresh-air-fund time.I take five between battles beside a mother with two daughters, who are playing on the rocks; we offer smiles and some light banter. She tells me I have some solid moves and asks how long I've been a Jedi. I tell her about sixteen years—since I have two other older sons.

"I have to tell you how nice it is to see a dad really get in there and mix it up with his kids. I mean, you even bring extra lightsabers and get other kids into the game? That's beyond the call."

I shake my head. "Once a camp director, always a camp director. Anyway, it's fun and keeps me from going brittle and seeding out be-fore my time."

We sit and watch as my sons bring her daughters some sabers and they scale the rocks.

"Well, it's rare . . . no matter what you think." She hesitates. "And I'm not their mother. I'm the aunt. They're my brother-in-law's kids. If just once I could see a lightsaber in his hand."

I smile, pick up my saber, because I have never been good at sit-ting when there's the need for a Darth Vader or Sith Lord to balance out the games. "It's nice that you bring them to the park, though. Does he travel a lot?"

She motions with her head. "He's sitting right over there."

Across the bridge, past the wood chip path, and out to the curb . . . sits BMW Guy. Christ on a Crooked Crutch . . . it's him. The Bluetooth, the license plate, the hand gesturing while he talks to the air above the steering wheel.

So many possible actions cross my mind. Sneak up behind the Beamer and place the red lightsaber across his throat while I ask him to step out of the vehicle and join my children and his for a show-down. A frontal attack with the saber à la Johnny Depp, *Pirates of the Caribbean?*

In the end it's too real and heartbreaking to do anything but sigh, shake my head, and feel the tangles of lost opportunities growing thick and wild around me like an invasive species. It would take more than a plastic lightsaber with a handy belt clip to cut through to this guy. I want to pity him but that's a cruel emotion, too.

So I go play with his children and light a candle for him in the playhouse of my mind.

As we pull past on the cargo bike I give him a wave, no glove this time, just a simple wave like the sort we'd offer on long stretches of New Mexico back roads to strangers who could be friends at the next pull-in or lifelines if the road grows teeth . . . and I hope, sincerely, that something breaks open and it becomes clear to him, some how, some way, that cars don't hug back and the stuff you want, get, and eventually walk away from, well, it's the least of it.

Chapter 21

BRING ON
THE NIGHT

Another rule of Bike Club, if you want to stay alive on two wheels: You don't ride at night. It's a solid rule backed up by all manner of alarming statistics. The irony being that if you want to feel most alive in the saddle, nothing beats pedaling into the darkness.

Few sensations in this world compare to carving the shadows of a blind curve under a full moon, timing the lights to coast an empty boulevard through the small of the night, or dancing on the pedals down that long black road, shielded in complete darkness.

It's womb-like, one of those secrets you want to keep. Night riding is stealing from a deep place. You might not get caught this time or the next, but keep pedaling the night road and it's only a matter of time before it takes you to the other side. That's why I don't ride at night. Except when I ride at night . . .

The first night ride I remember was right after I heard Springsteen perform "Darkness on the Edge of Town" live in Tampa, Florida, circa 1980.

It was the middle of the night when we hauled our bikes out of the bushes. Like everyone else, we'd waited too long after Bruce—sweating, spent, completely emptied of all his gargantuan gifts and rebel soul—called it quits. We stood there in the darkness with our newfound rock-'n'-roll brothers and sisters, refusing at first to believe the service was over, then pounding the backs of the seats and stomping the cement floor, willing it to go on, and finally standing together in the silence, desperate, a little pathetic, not able to let go yet.

We had to make sure that the four-hour religious experience of sound and fury we'd just come through was truly in the books.

We needed to see the body one more time . . . and it wouldn't have hurt if someone'd stepped up to the mike and told us what all this stirred-around shit inside our heads and guts meant, but as with most things in life, we were unceremoniously shown the door. The mass of humanity moved in unison, heading out of the civic center in that subdued, post-concert, ear-ringing zombie shuffle through the breezeway out to the parking lot.

And the whole time I kept thinking, *Four fucking hours, for less than ten dollars, plus those stoners in the El Camino gave us free beer. I may have just peaked.*

For too long I measured concert experiences against that evening. It wasn't until Tom Petty that the perfect combination of company, Red Stripe beer, a poor-ventilation concert floor contact high, and a hat trick encore—"Refugee," "American Girl," and "Breakdown"— recalibrated things a little.

In the bigger scheme, though, The Boss is the most luscious, bittersweet way to lose one's live-music virginity. It ruined me, really. But would I trade it for love or money? Ironic that one of my favorite old man Glory Days memories will more than likely be about the guy who popularized Glory Days memories.

Sure, I'd seen the Eagles the summer before, during an outdoor show at Tampa stadium, but that didn't count; dry humping with your jeans still on, if that. Years later, when Jeff Bridges, as the Dude in *The Big Lebowski*, tells the cabdriver to play anything but the Eagles, I let loose with such a freakishly loud laugh that Beth peered over the darkened theater at me like I was touched. Fucking Eagles. Am I right, Donnie?

Five of us pedaling out of the lot together. As we went, mostly in silence, one would peel off, then another, until it was only John Greene coasting the empty streets beside me.

John would take a decidedly different path than me later in life, but at that moment we were bound tightly to each other by The Boss.

Live oak trees heavy with Spanish moss along both sides of the avenues formed something of a tunnel. The streetlights gave the moss a luminous quality. I rode with no hands, no helmet, and a new concert T-shirt.

I've never felt so safe, so sure.

The night air in southern Florida can hold an entire day. Heavy with conversations and sunscreen and hope and rage, blotted with schemes and come-ons and scams and second acts and resignation and mouthfuls of sand and seagulls and always the hint of salt drifting in off the bay. It holds everything close and low, like a dead man's last moan, until the pressure shifts at dawn. Then every surface is wet without notice. But sometimes, like sorrow, it's too heavy to let go of yet. It bottles right into the next morning and through to the next, until it breaks wide, shatters down in a furious afternoon monsoon.

The thing about my young life on that silent Florida night was that I didn't have any real secrets yet, certainly nothing worth hiding inside the humidity of the evening. Nada. I'm certain I postured as if I did, but no . . . nothing more than imaginary crimes and future accomplishments, Supertramp lyrics, an angry Clash chorus, and what I approximated my first real girlfriend's nipples looked like based only on the shape and feel established briefly while making out behind a Shakey's pizza parlor.

Closest I could come to a secret was that I liked to jot down openings to stories if only to get them to stop rattling around inside my head. I might do something with them in the future . . . if I remembered, but that was a way off, down a distant, still-dark road.

I felt deeply. I just didn't have a clue what it was I was feeling yet.

But those four hours with Springsteen were an unequivocal victory. There would be other triumphs and harmonic convergences— Little Feat, Thin Lizzy, Jackson Browne, Led Zeppelin. Not Queen, though. I could have seen Freddie and the boys in the (glammed-up) flesh, but, like an asshole who thinks there will always be more time in this world, I waved away the offer during fifth period one Thursday. I decided instead to pick up an extra shift at the shoe store and catch the opening of *Rocky II* playing two doors down from the store. Stallone chasing a chicken around rather than downing raw eggs during the training montage scenes this time, but it was basically the same movie as *Rocky*.

The night broke easy and spilled its secrets down in the form of a light, warm rain. Water hummed off my back tire. I leaned in, letting beads of water coming off the Spanish moss cool my face. I studied the pavement a few feet ahead of my front wheel, attempting to block out all the big houses and wide, thick lawns. Those landmarks that indicated I was almost home.

I loved the physical contours of Florida too much to stay. The mangroves, the inlets, the sand hills and palmetto groves. Like watching a family member waste away from addiction or, worse, a cancer with no cure. At least with addiction there's a chance at redemption. I lived among the very people hastening its demise. The builders and bankers and backers blacktopping paradise. I wasn't even aware at that age how much it hurt me to stand and watch it happen. I just knew I felt something more than garden-variety teenage angst. I knew it was about more than me this time. But then doesn't every teenager believe their angst is singular, special? Larger than the world. It's sort of the textbook definition of angst.

How I'd get out, or even if I would, was an open question, but if home is about acceptance, I wasn't ready to give in, listen for the sound of settling, and receive the cash and prizes that come from hugging the familiar while looking away. And if I stayed, at some point I wouldn't just be watching the destruction anymore but actively participating in it.

Parking my bicycle in the garage, I squirreled away an idea, something that would turn out to be the most important secret I could have stumbled upon, a blurry vision of the future that altered the course of my days. I turned back to my bike as it fell against rakes and bags of empty soda cans, the back wheel spinning for a while on its own. I looked at it hard. What I was thinking was something along the lines of: *We're just getting started.* Or maybe *Oh, the places we will go.*

In hindsight I was just trying to see my way out. Somehow I knew the bike would help me get on with it, give me the strength to opt for experiences over shiny stuff and soft easy landings. Travel light and fast and free. A real hobo epiphany in the darkness. But rather than a steamer or railcar, my ticket out of town would be a bicycle.

I knew it was only a matter of time. I would have to run (or pedal), just like Bruce instructed, because, well, you know, to do anything else was a suicide rap.

My teenage brain, flooded with echoing reverb, testosterone, confusion, and hope, hadn't caught up with my heart. So it was translating my thoughts into something basic and stripped down. I just needed a mantra I could get behind.

As I reached up for the chain on the garage light, I was hit with that new-shirt smell, amplified by the rain it had soaked up. I wanted to feel wet and hungry and tired rather than air-conditioned, pampered, and waited on. I just wanted to feel something beyond these gated communities.

Pulling the chain, I stood in the dark and uttered a simple phrase said by teenagers down through generations, since the first caveman's son grabbed a handful of fire and stormed out on his wheel . . .

"Fuck this town."

Chapter 22

FAREWELL
TO A FRIEND

Alejandro Alverez had a way of moving a bicycle so effortlessly that, even though I stood half a foot taller than him, he dwarfed me with his skills. My friend from Monterrey, Mexico, rode like it was the first and last time he might own a pair of legs. I hated him a little for that. But he seemed to live as effortlessly as he rode and for that I loved Alejandro as one loves a brother from another mother. I featured him in the final chapter of *Riding Outside the Lines*, and tried, but surely failed, to learn much from his style.

We met on a mountain bike adventure high in the hills above Puerto Vallarta. Alejandro and Chiquis were our guides for the week. When I asked why they weren't taking the small airplane of questionable mechanical repute the next morning, Chiquis mumbled something about being attached to living for another day, but it was Alejandro who offered up the real reason: "Because I want to get in a warm-up ride."

Sweet weeping Jesus, that warm-up ride involved pedaling uphill while we flew, not metaphorically, but actually flew to the starting point. When Alejandro arrived not ten minutes behind the last panic-stricken shuttle of tourists and bicycles, many of whom were kissing the ground after disembarking the Cessna, I knew I wanted to hang with my guides more than any of the guests.

"When did you start?" I asked.His smile was the size of the world. "Today."

Autumn in the mountain town of San Sebastian, high up on "La buffa," is almost heaven. We were relaxing in what was still John Huston's villa. Lit only by hurricane lamps and a fat harvest moon, we decided to hike out to a cornfield where a flatbed truck missing its wheels, but featuring a working radio, provided a comfortable bed to view the stars. We passed around some herb and concurred that even Mexican radio stations overplay the Eagles.

By the end of the week the three of us were joined at the hip. On a long climb, just to show me how strong he was, Alejandro would talk during the push to the top of the switchback. And though he would not have been confused for a New Age facilitator, at that moment he did ask me what animal I would compare my riding style to.

"El Gato" but only because that it was one of the few animal names I knew how to say in Spanish and to say in one quick breath. He knew as much, laughing so hard I was able to pass him for a few yards. When this racer, once ranked number one in Mexico, caught up, Alejandro looked me in the eye, gave me a keen smile, and said, "No, no, my friend. I ride like El Gato. I float and glide and pedal lightly and land on my feet. You? More like El Armadillo."

On the downhill, back in earshot, I yelled, "The world needs armadillos, you know!"

Last week, when someone emailed me the link to that article and horrific photo of the tragedy in which a Texas man killed a cyclist and injured ten more in a drunk-driving nightmare at a bicycle race in Mexico, I did what most of you who saw it did.

I wrung my hands, felt a piece of myself sag, and even though it is not my daily practice, I said a silent prayer for the dead. Then I read the name of the cyclist who had been killed. Then his age and his hometown.

Respect for the passing of an anonymous fellow cyclist had just become very personal. The bottom fell out of my heart. I desperately needed to put some speed in the saddle, some velocity to help outpace my anger and dull this loss.

When I told Alejandro I thought he was bigger than Mexico's race scene, that he could be a player on the world stage, he'd just smiled: "You know, I used to sell crap to tourists at the airport. We are friends now so I say to you it's a nice idea, this growing beyond Mexico, but it won't sell for someone like me, someone from here . . . not today, maybe not ever."

I like to think that the reason Alejandro was the one cyclist out of 420 racers who got his ticket punched that day is because he was the one out front, always floating and gliding and making it look effortless.

Forever young and always going very, very fast.

Chapter 23

DESPITE ALL OUR (ROAD) RAGE . . .

Next on NPR's *Morning Edition*: "Investing the time and energy in the coming years to cultivate and improve your tech relationship with your car . . . as it gets smarter and more complex."

Really? This sounds like a nightmare of Orwellian proportions.

As I pull on bike gloves I find it necessary to talk back to the radio.

"Unplug yourself before it's too late. Ride a bicycle that hasn't fundamentally changed in a hundred years, and cultivate relationships in person, with other human beings. Jesus, the only high-tech connection I want with a car—when I have to use one—is getting the Curtis Mayfield tunes balanced just right between the front and back speakers."

And with that I pedal onto the battlefield that is America's roadways.

A distracted Lexus driver rolled the crosswalk *and* the stop sign in a school zone while on her cell phone, slamming her brakes inches from our bike train and Matteo's knees. A shiny, unyielding bumper tagged the back edge of my rear wheel. I felt the bike fishtail from the impact but I kept it upright. She put up a hand to indicate that my terror needed to wait for a second while she finished the call.

I went from abject horror and certainty that we would be crushed to a sick-in-my-stomach fury. Her sheepish grin wasn't gonna cut it. I pulled the bike and ourselves from around the bumper and spoke in an Eastwood whisper-growl into her window.

"In your sealed compartment you may have missed the sound of my son screaming! All the money you are rushing off to make or spend wouldn't bring my family back. Using a school zone as a short-cut to work or coffee is a shit-the-bed bad idea."

She isn't grinning anymore.

"I have memorized your plate." Still in whisper-growl mode. "And if I ever see that phone in your ear while you're operating a three-thousand-pound piece of machinery through a school zone I will hunt you down and throw it into the Willamette River." She starts to cry. I lean in a bit closer, all whisper now, and suggest that she marries that emotion, stores it up, and pulls it out for a moment or two every time she starts her car in the morning. I ride into the schoolyard shaky and flushed. It had to be said and perhaps it will stick, but I don't feel victorious. But kissing my boy into the rest of his day, both of us still whole and upright, was a win nonetheless.

I will say that what kept me from grabbing her phone on the spot and crushing it to pieces or telling her to pick it up at the principal's office after school . . . I didn't have bail money.

A massive Dodge Ram was forced to remain at the stop sign while a pack of bike dads pedaled through the intersection in front of their bumper, and then into the bike lane on the other side of the street. As the parade of parents and kids in the saddle passed, the driver revved and lurched its gargantuan bumper forward a little, coming within a foot or two of the bikes, and I noted a child of about six flinching. When that didn't get the proper rise out of the dad convoy, the truck honked. I could hear laughter inside the cab.

I waited alongside the truck since I was going in their direction. The passenger of the truck decides he needs to roll down the window and ask me something. "Hey, tell me something, where did the real men go? All of you driving your little hippie toys now. You're everywhere." The driver laughs. I laugh, too, nod, and offer the following rebuttal. "Actually, you don't drive a bike. You have to use muscles, reflexes, balance, and sweat . . . shit like that. Real men shit. Far as I can tell driving involves sitting on a moving couch, turning wheels, pressing buttons and pedals, and jerking on sticks. Same stuff preschoolers do with plastic toys while watching Elmo." Yep, I can be a right proper prick, but it felt good to hear them choke on a few swear words, tossed in my general direction without much enthusiasm. Give 'em this much, veterans of locker room trash talking, they knew when a solid kick to the head had been administered.

I left them to chewing on that, and licking their wounds, still stuck at the stop sign because a line of cars had formed a petro-belching parade of traffic, barring their way into or through the intersection a bit longer, while we rounded the corner and pedaled away.

My upraised clenched fist, the cyclist's finish-line victory salute, was uncalled for, but I closed it out with a peace sign.

I rolled Sawyer home from preschool to discover that there was another type of class I needed to attend, the one where I was called by my conscience to school the Neanderthal in his behemoth black truck the size of Texas idling plumes of diesel in front of the

Montessori school across the street from my house.

I try for the live-and-let-live approach on and off the bike, peace signs and waves when people shout things like get the hell off *my* road or worse, but after watching the truck idle there another five minutes, I could not abide. I explained that since my kids would be playing in the yard now, bringing the number of kids sucking fumes to around twenty within a few feet of his truck, if he planned on sitting there with his engine running for more than another ten seconds, I'd need him to turn off the engine. He grunted and went back to his paperwork and kept idling. I stepped over to the truck window. "I'm asking nicely, but we can go another way."

He sighed. "Or what, you'll run me over with your bike, libtard?"

I pulled out my camera. "Or I'll take a photo of your business magnet and license plate and let my thousands of friends on social media know exactly which business is gassing our five-year-olds." He turned off his engine.

When people hear about these run-ins, they'll ask if it's bikes versus cars for me. I find this laughable.

"You're thinking too small. It's nature versus concrete! It's us against our unchecked appetites. It's the woods versus the shop windows. Cars? Just the tip of the iceberg."

Edward Abbey summed up what's been while lost rolling around inside our cages, and how we might find our way back.

how dare you imprison little children in your
goddamned upholstered horseless hearse?
Yes sir, yes madam, I entreat you, get out of

those motorized wheelchairs, get off your
foam rubber backsides, stand up straight like
men! like women! like human beings! and
walk—walk—WALK upon our sweet and
blessed land!

—Edward Abbey, *Desert Solitaire* (1968)

Chapter 24

THE MOTHER OF ALL TAILWINDS

Bringing one hundred miles in under three hours on a bicycle is akin to breaking the three-minute mile on foot. Maybe the pros do it all the time, I'm not one of them so I wouldn't know, but if you don't have a resting heart rate below fifty and a fat to body mass index of 5 percent, charging past the hundred-mile mark in three hours is a pipe dream . . .

Monks could use the climb out of Yosemite as a form of self-flagellation. Once on top, though, few places outside Vegas pay off as big. I pointed my wheels toward Pinedale and never looked back. Feathering the brakes as little as possible on a steep descent is a dodgy proposition. Pressing hard on luck, relying on muscle memory, the lines I was choosing down that mountain road resembled extreme downhill skiing.

I have no idea what it looked like from the cheap seats—a fully loaded touring bicycle and rider blitzing off a mountain, leaning into the curves, defying gravity and common sense, yelping a primal howl into the morning light, but with fifteen hundred miles of West Coast up-and-down riding behind me, I was capable of doing things on a bicycle that would have me in traction if I tried them now.

One of the feel-good philosophers said that life's a sliver of light between two infinities of darkness, and I say that within that, it's a few precious moments of grace and daring that let us see it through and offer something beautiful to talk about in the closing scenes.

The downhill run off Yosemite makes my best-of list, hands down. Something unexpected happened at the bottom of the mountain. I didn't encounter a series of rollers to break my spirit or throw off my rhythm, I didn't turn directions and head into the wind, I didn't experience a slight tilting of the earth in favor of the away team. Instead, I kept going at a breakneck pace, aided by a slight downhill, something almost undetectable by the naked eye, and a tailwind that grew stronger as the miles dropped away.

When a gift as big as this comes your way you jump to it no matter what your body did the day before. Mine had climbed Half Dome and should have been putting up siren wails of protest, but my systems seemed to be on the same page as my desire. I ran through all the reasons to slow down, but came up wanting.

A spot of yellow in the distance kept growing until it became a school bus. I closed in on its back end the way a torpedo does in war movies. I assumed it was because the bus was making stops, but when I got close enough to see the faces of middle school kids in the very back seats, I was doing thirty-eight miles an hour and the bus was rolling steady. That's when they put up the sign. No, not the one that would have, by law, forced me to come to a complete stop—something I don't think I could have done, either physically or emotionally. This was a handmade sign done in Magic Markers: NO MORE TEACHERS, NO MORE BOOKS!

Another popped up: SEE YOU NEXT YEAR, SUCKERS!

And one more: SCHOOL'S OUT FOREVER!

And then the one you couldn't get away with these days even in middle school: SCHOOL'S BEEN BLOWN 2 PIECES!

I did the math as I hummed Alice Cooper's anthem to summertime anarchy sung from coast to coast this time of year. It was indeed the last day of servitude and those signs were the smallest act of rebellion, maybe their first: hiding out in the back of a bus, showing off over the release from indenture just a few hours before it really happened.

Hell, what can they do to us now?

I gave them a nod and a smile as I got within spitting distance—it was like looking through a fun-house mirror back at my middle school self. I'd have bet the farm that half the bus was carrying Silly String or cans of shaving cream, and that seeing a bike going forty miles per hour in the sunshine of a June morning was a glimpse at what could be . . . possibilities. Hang on, kids, the world is waiting for you on the other side of the glass.

At first they were making faces and trying to be fierce, but once the sign holders saw that I was keeping up with their bus, their expressions changed.

Remarkable as it sounds, I began to overtake the rig. Drafting it at first, à la that scene from the film *Breaking Away*. The sign kids were fist-pumping me on to victory. Maybe it was when the rest of the busload of kids urged me forward with high-pitched cheers and the lowering of those undersized windows, but I found myself halfway to the front mirrors, then even with the passenger door. Cheers grew as I gained ground on the front of the vehicle. In my mirror I saw children's hands and heads wedging out the side windows now. The driver looked stunned. We made eye contact through the glass of the passenger door. I gave a little shrug and kept going. At least he had an answer to why his cargo had suddenly morphed into *Lord of the Flies*.

At some point the bus turned off Highway 41, but not before I had a quarter mile on it. That should have been enough. I'd outpaced a bus for God's sake, but it only fueled my need for speed. We're not even talking about speed here, but a desire to break from everything that binds us to ourselves. I wanted to time-travel, to find a place inside the ride that doesn't exist anywhere else. World-class surfers, when asked if anything compares to catching the perfect wave, have said they've felt the edges of it on long bike rides.

I put my head down and went all the way inside.

When I came out, my CatEye had clocked 102 miles. It was 10:20 a.m. I'd been at it for two hours and fifty-seven minutes. My legs and lungs were brand new.

The silence by the side of the road felt complete. I looked back for the first time. A breeze blew hot on my face. The three-hour century was part of my personal history now. Done. The only part of it that would come to matter would be the memory of how it made me feel. I owned the stopwatch now.

There was a turnoff for a recreation area two hundred yards back. I pedaled slowly at first, then something took over. I fought into the wind, stood and hammered to get my pace up, before realization washed over me. I geared down and dug for it, struggling by the campground at under ten miles an hour.

Call me the king of pain, I'd decided to double down. A place twenty-five miles back had caught my eye in the split second it took to rocket by the first time. A place where you could pan for gold and sleep in a replica of a prairie schooner.

Speed's tricky. We try to harness it to serve us, to save us, but when we realize it's taken over the show, it's often too late.

Those twenty-five miles ate up another three hours, but I'd be damned if I was going to put up a tent and call it a day at ten in the morning; not with wagons and the lure of gold waiting back up the road. Not with blacktop and a daylight in front of me.

Besides, since conquering time and space, I set the pace from here on in, and do things that matter to me with the time that remains.

Chapter 25

EVERYTHING I REALLY NEED TO KNOW I LEARNED IN A BROOKS SADDLE

All I really need to know about how to live and what to do and how to be, I learned by climbing into the saddle of a bicycle and riding it as far as it would take me.

Thought I was going to pull the mother of all acts of plagiarism and say kindergarten? No disrespect to Robert Fulghum, who inspired this little ode to the bicycle as a guide to better global citizenship, but I was too busy eating paste and running away from cooties dispensed by Diane "Future Miss Pennsylvania" Gillespie to pick up much useful knowledge from the six-and-under set. Now, colds, I picked up plenty of those in kindergarten. My other book would be titled *All I Ever Need to Know About the Immune System I Learned in Kindergarten.*

Alas, wisdom was not waiting for me in the sandbox, only a nasty piece of work named Bobby Hicks and his Tonka-truck-wielding acts of violence. (Ritalin was years away.) Nor, as an adult, did I drive toward nirvana behind the wheel of a Chevy, Ford, or even rickshaw (though we drove a long way to see Nirvana in a Toyota Corolla during the summer of 1992).

All I really need to know about how to navigate life starts and ends with the soothing meditations of a perfectly timed cadence.

Here's what I've learned at the University of Brooks and a few field courses at the College of Campagnolo:

• Share Everything

The road, the draft you've been sucking off your ride partner for the past ten miles, those extra Clif Bars (not just the flavors you can barely choke down, but the ones that taste like Scooby Snacks to a bonking cyclist). Share the best route home (for sunsets, wide shoulders, animal sightings, a car only every few minutes, the one that gives you a descent *and* a straightaway on the final push to your doorstep).

Share that extra tube you lug along on every ride (just remember to replace it before your next shot out the gate because that's the second your path will be laced with glass and goat heads and you'll no doubt curse your generosity and my name). Share what you see on the road ahead with others behind you, figuratively and literally. (I once called out "glass on your left" followed by "Why Canada will always feel superior in winter sports and comedy to us on your right." We were cycling by a 120-foot-long hockey stick and two-thousand-pound puck statue outside the Hall of Fame in Minnesota. I think it was Minnesota. It looked like a Coen brothers film set.)

But most of all, share your love of cycling—not only for the beautiful lines, curves, simple design elegance, and earth-friendly features of a device once called a bone-shaker, but also for what it does for your physical health and mental state, where it can take you in terms of possibilities, and at a tempo that, while it might not actually stop time, is the closest thing to a fountain of youth on this planet or any other. Hey, there's a reason both you an Einstein look so much alike on a bicycle. It's called wonder . . . and Helmet Hair.

• Don't Hit

A curb if you want true wheels and round rims, railroad tracks at anything but a right angle if you want to stay upright, or car doors as they are being opened by a distracted driver if you want to stay out of the hospital. Bicycles offer object lessons in momentum (it's your friend all of the time), velocity (it's your out-of-control lover who at some point will rocket you to a place where you are frightened and thrilled and calling out for your mommy simultaneously), and gravity (it has no friends and should not be trusted—respected but not trusted—especially in the curves, around black ice, or whenever you've forgotten those gloves with the good padding in them). Bicycles show us how important it is to avoid life's collisions.

• Hydrate or Die

There's no deeper meaning with this one, no social context or larger vision, just drink up or die, more . . . go ahead and tip back the water bottle as often as you can. Sure, they had juice in kindergarten and showed us all where the water fountain was, but it took a long bike ride in July, cramps, and doing the cockroach complete with kicking leg muscle spasms on my back, all while licking the last hint of moisture from the inside of a water bottle lid, to bring this message home.

• **Play Fair**

Forget the constitution or the United Nations, the bicycle is the most democratic device in the world. It levels the field, any field. Anyone can learn to ride. You don't have to be Tour de France fast to enjoy it; in fact it's more fun if you have something to lose (weight, seconds off your best time, a cubicle job you've just ridden away from). When you get onto a bicycle, no matter who you are, race and class peel away, possessions boil down to what you can carry in a few bags, and you turn back into a ten-year-old giving everyone around you the benefit of the doubt.

• **The World Is Not Flat**

It's all about circles in this life—the ones you make with friends, with your choices, and with your cadence. Which is not to say there won't be bumps distorting these grand, geometric patterns. True story: Galileo was placed under house arrest by the Catholic Church in the 1600s for claiming the world was round and it revolved around the sun. It wasn't until 1992 that the church admitted it had that one wrong. So try to remember that the bike and its circles will always bring you back around . . . if you give it long enough.

• **Take a Nap Every Afternoon**

Preferably outside, beside your bike. And if you can swing it, by a stream, under a willow tree, or in a cornfield with the breeze making the stalks hum ever so slightly. Perhaps in a pasture outside a vineyard after you've sampled a bit of the grape, or on a bench under the shade of a country store porch. Maybe under a small-town post office awning. These are power naps, these are naps you'll savor and search for and call out to at 2 a.m. on a sleepless Wednesday back home.

• Clean Up Your Own Mess

Dead men tell no tales, but greasy hands from chain repairs and bike maintenance leave a trail of stains Hansel could follow in a snowstorm . . . and a look of divorce in your mate's eyes. The proper care of a bicycle and keeping track of all its little parts that will roll under a desk or into a heating vent can make even the most pigpen among us into part-time neat freaks. Being anal even 10 percent of the time has saved more than one marriage.

• Wash Your Hands Before You Eat

(See the one about grease and whatnot.)

• Warm Milk and Cold Cookies Are Good for You

Or in our case, warm Gatorade, cold pasta out of a ziplock hanging over your handlebar bag while riding, and ice cream are good for you. Cycling dispels the notion that everything in life has to be the perfect temperature, completely dry, always easy and without pain . . . as long as there's a bit of ice cream waiting for us, cyclists will abide.

• When You Go Out in the World, Watch Out for Traffic, Hold Hands, and Stick Together

I don't know how well the holding-hands part translates to cycling (though I have seen the Dutch accomplish this in transit without much trouble, those dexterous bastards of windmill country). I do know from traffic and cycling that in life we must presume we are invisible and make a show of our days. It's the only way to have sleep-walkers snap out of it for a second and notice lives being pedaled a little less ordinary. It's the only way our ideas will see the light of day and we won't get crushed by every other one of us locked in rolling steel cages bombarded by shock-jock rhetoric vaguely angered by how we ended up in this place and space to begin with. Cycling has taught me this: Inside every car . . . is a person who really needs a bike ride.

It's made me want to light up the world while I'm here. Bright-colored clothing, creative thoughts, spotlights on the handlebars shining on unpopular ideas that you know in your gut to be right or you think are worth exploring. And reflective tape, lots of reflective tape. That and changing things in your own life before asking others to do the same. Flashing lights, too, are even better than flashy jerseys. And of course crash-tested headgear if you want to stick around for the rest of the party.

About sticking together—what's a pace line or a party without friends? I'll answer my own question: It's a two-wheeled cross-country angst-filled vision quest by a college sophomore taking a "break," complete with dog-eared copy of Edward Abbey's *Desert Solitaire*.

When this cat has had enough to think, the bike ride will sweat out much of the angst, leaving a few ounces of clarity to question and act on his future.

• Look

Look around. That goes double for cyclists—too many times we put our heads down and just work the little circles with our pedals all the way home. Resist this temptation if you want to enjoy the ride on and off the bike. Look for an escape clause when things get too much for you, open it up, and ride like the devil is on your heels . . . it will feel good. No, it will feel better than that, it will feel like sleeping outside for the first time and waking up alive at first light, like a mother's embrace, a promise kept between tomorrow and the creative powers of the universe. In the end there's just the myth of escape anyway. Only an exchange of one set of difficulties for another. No one outpaces their own imperfections, but it's a lot of fun to give them a good race. Know that no matter how far you ride, eventually you will need to find something to ride to or the bicycle, just like any obsession, will swallow you whole.

• We All Fall Down

Everyone and everything falls down eventually: Twin Towers, the Roman Empire (most of it anyway, except for the ruins on the official tour), Kurt Vonnegut, rest in peace my hopeful cynic. Truth is, the more you worry about crashing, the more likely it is you will. Riding and living tentatively is the kiss of . . . well, you know. Worse still, if you try to eliminate the chance of crashing, it's the kiss of mediocrity. Over time you'll go brittle while barely noticing, and your bike will grow cobwebs from hanging in the garage or hiding in the basement. Try this, act as if today is the last day you'll own a set of legs . . . it might be. No, I haven't heard anything, but if I had, I'd want what you would want . . . one more ride.

Chapter 26

SWIMMING IN A TOILET FOR $200, ALEX!

As Beth likes to point out, it's many things, but being a member of our family is never boring. When it threatens to head in that direction, the best remedy is to get on our bikes and ride.

We spent four carefree summer days pedaling down the Oregon coast. This is not to say that assuming the position in the saddles wipes away all stress and takes you to a magical land, but it always changes up the family vibe for the better. It works our bodies and literally changes everyone's perspective. Our destination a producer friend's beach house near Florence, Oregon. Sand boarding, hiking, cruising the hard packed sand on our bikes, flying kites behind us . . . mellow family time.

Keeping the festive atmosphere alive, on the next long stretch of road, I green-lighted a beachfront hotel complete with in-room Jacuzzi and a heated pool overlooking the beach, only yards from the waves. After 9,000 miles of family cycling across the continent together, twice, I've learned that placing festive destinations along way keeps spirits high and avoids mutiny.

All this and more had been the promise of the Best Western Plus in Brookings. We talked about the heated pool just yards from the surf for the next hundred miles.

I chanced it something awful by not making reservations ahead of time, but we scored the last beachfront room anyway. Beth and the boys were in their swimsuits before I had the other panniers off the bikes. I told them I'd catch up.

About twenty minutes later I find a Rockwell scene out by the pool, if Rockwell had thought to paint swimmers on the West Coast. Okay, Hockney, then. I find a David Hockney vibe out by the pool, and I couldn't be happier.

There's something quite delicious about earning a swim after miles in the saddle. I almost cannonball in, but pause at the last moment, remembering to take off my glasses.

At the same moment Matteo giggle-yells, "Oh my God, look at this. Oh my God!"

I'm expecting a ladybug he's mistaken for a bee or a *MAD* magazine someone has left poolside. I almost ignore and jump, but I'm won over by his enthusiasm just one more time. He brings me over to the shallow end. Could it be? I frantically scan above me for a tree bearing pinecones . . . no luck.

That's poop! Not one, two, or three logs, but *five logs* of dookie! Imagine an alarm on the decibel level of a Three Mile Island meltdown going off inside my head.

My eyes dart around the entire pool area, and this is what they take in. Beth floating on her back . . . lazy, happy. Sawyer is all the way underwater exploring with his goggles. Matteo is wet head-to-toe.

My family has been swimming in a toilet for nearly half an hour!

"Those aren't pinecones!" I scream.

I wave my hands like I'm flagging down traffic in the fog even though Beth is no more than five yards away.

"Out! Everyone out! The pool is full of poo! The pool is full of poo!"

I'm the Paul Revere of pool safety.

Beth's expression goes from harmony with the world and the calm center of her summer vacation as a hardworking schoolteacher, to disgusted panic.

And here's the ridiculous part . . . as a dad, my first reaction is to grab paper towels and reach in to *clean* out someone else's poop! I get one piece deckside, like it's a drowning victim. That's when my eyes meet Beth's. She gives me a look. If I could, I would have given myself the very same look.

"What in God's name am I doing?"

Sawyer surfaces. Curious, he swims over to the poo area with his head down, searching his world through his goggles.

"No, Sawyer!"

I reach in, arm in the water to my elbow, and pull him out and plop him deckside in one fluid motion.

Beth rushes all three of them to the hotel room for Defcon Level 5 sanitizing!

"Towels. Get more towels!" Her parting order.

I'm on my way to the lobby. It's eight people deep in there—everyone hoping for a room on the beach as the holiday weekend approaches. This side of yelling "Fire!" in a movie theater, try announcing "Oh my God, you need to know that there are five logs of poo in your pool and my family has been swimming in there for twenty minutes!"

They ask me to calm down, but you can see the panic on the reception staff's faces.

"You try being calm when your family's been swimming in a toilet!" I say.

"We're on it!" the woman behind the counter says, and she means it. I hear walkie-talkies coming to life, bells ringing, and a buzzer bringing someone out from a backroom. I go back to my own room to get myself clean and see how the family is dealing.

I fume throughout the cleaning process. I've paid a heap of money to put my family in a toilet! And now all the beachside swimming and floating in the pool we had planned is shot.

Beth steps out of the shower, looks at me, and says, "You know how I wish you'd be less excitable sometimes? Well, not this time!"

I'd say there's shit-eating grin on my face as I walk toward the lobby, but that's too close to home for the situation. It makes more sense to say that the manager does not see the shitstorm heading his/her way. Hurricane Joe is about to make landfall.

It's interesting, when I'm given permission to get excited, I actually achieve a state of Zen-like calm. What was a Grand Central Station lobby a few minutes before is now a ghost town. The staffer at the desk smiles like a helium-based greeter at Outback Steakhouse.

"I totally understand what you need, and the manager is on his way."

Haven't said a word yet. I take a seat, smile, and moments later I'm greeted by Magnum PI, if he'd let himself go on a twenty-year pub crawl up and down the West Coast after the series ended.

There's the Hawaiian shirt, the caterpillar mustache gone gray. He reminds me of that uncle who, with no explanation from your parents, stayed in the guest room for a week or two every other spring. He's the type of guy who has managed to piece together several decades of patchy employment, but truly, he's at least another decade removed from giving a fuck. He offers me a weak handshake.

"Let's talk in the conference room." He has a pad of paper and a pen. I feel a little like we're late for a timeshare seminar. Magnum opens with, "We have a pool attendant, not a guard but an attendant in the summer, and of all days, she called in sick."

"Of all days," I repeat back. We both nod a few times.

"Look, I understand you're shocked about the pool and these things happen, but my family was talking about the pool on the beach for a hundred miles and now we won't be going back in it for twenty-four hours—one of those logs had lost its structural integrity—so in point of fact, I've paid you to let them swim around in a toilet for half an hour."

He purses his lips.

"What can you do for me?"

Magnum sets the pad down on the table.

"I'd upgrade you right now, but I'm out of the suites. What about cutting your room price in half for tonight?" He nods like he's ordering us up a pair of imaginary drinks. I shake my head.

"I think you've missed the boat here. Unless the *plus* in your corporate sign stands for discomfort, panic, and hazmat-level experiences at no extra charge. If it weren't so late and we weren't on bicycles, I'd be cashing out and heading down the road with a horrible Yelp review in the works. As it is, with my following of readers, this will make it on FB and probably into a book somewhere. Oh, and I'm gonna need the name and policy number of your insurance company—we're headed for a family reunion and God help you guys if my family gets sick in the next twenty-four hours. So I ask again, what are you going to do for me to see that this gets a happy ending?"

Oh, and I'll take that imaginary drink now.

Magnum is nothing if not a man of the street. He gets it or he's just too tired to fight. Either way he comes back with a sincere smile, nods, and leans back in the conference chair.

"You are absolutely right, I don't know what I was thinking. The room is comped, here's my card in case anything does come up with your family's health, and please take this code so that the next time you come through you can stay with us for free . . ." He looks at me to see if this will be enough. "In the upgraded suite, of course."

That night we pedaled our bikes in circles across the hard packed sand, yards from the crashing surf under a nearly full moon, shooting roman candles—leftovers from the 4th of July—into the night sky and at each other. The laughter that filled the darkness was loose and outsized and laced with abandon. It was the laughter of the creatures in Where The Wild Things Are.

The vacation had three more poop-related experiences, an occupational hazard of raising boys, but none involving logs in a pool. At the end of our travels I turned to Beth.

"That was quite a shitty vacation!"

Of course, we're already packing the panniers and planning next summer's ride.

Chapter 27

SIGNS THAT CYCLING HAS TAKEN OVER YOUR LIFE (YOU SAY THIS AS IF IT'S A BAD THING?)

"Hello, my name is Joe . . ."

"Hello, Joe."

"And I'm a cycling addict. It's been ten days since I clipped in, twenty more since I checked my CatEye, and a full month since I bought something I did not need off the clearance table at my local bike shop."

Okay, so I've never been forced to make this confession, but if there really were a 12-step program for addicts of adventures on two wheels, friends and family would have tackled me to the ground years ago. Except for things like, say, a job, or sleep, meals, and the occasional social contact with people, there's really nothing stopping any of us from dreaming, thinking, scheming, or actually cycling twenty-four seven . . . or close to it.

Of course it would be utter folly for you to push away from that desk you've been riding like a little corporate jockey all these years.

Foolishness of the highest order for you to sublet the house or sell the farm and roll out the door for a world trek, or what about signing up for the local race series, cyclocross, or every century on this season's schedule? Life could get interesting in a hurry, God forbid. So while you contemplate a few of these rash choices I've littered your lane with, let's see just how over the edge you are with a little test.

(Full disclosure: Like any good test maker, I've compiled this pop quiz from many sources over the years—my twisted brain, websites, surveys, emails from friends—but most of it comes from cyclists in the act of pedaling, getting ready to pedal, or lying on the side of the blacktop after pedaling too far, too fast, or both. In other words, experts. I would like to thank them collectively for their inspired madness . . . Pedal, Forrest, pedal!)

Now, pencils ready . . .

Are You Addicted to Cycling?

Check Off All That Apply to You (bonus points for speed, deductions for drafting):

• You know every traffic light sequence in the tricounty area for stop-free pedaling.

• Either it's a Brooks saddle or I will stand and pedal the whole way, thank you.

• You wear more tights than a children's theater group performing *Peter Pan.*

• You have eaten pasta directly out of your front bag, while pedaling.

• You have more up-to-date knowledge of bike specs, gear, and camping equipment than the staff at your local shop, the reps in your community, and the editors at national magazines.

• You have a killer set of bodybuilder quads and a pair of angel-hair-pasta-thin arms. That ten-year-old boy called again. He wants his biceps back.

• You don't hate drivers as much as pity them in their steel cages, surrounded by shock-jock rhetoric and their vague anger over how it came to this.

• You think about each hill as a cyclist, even when you are driving in a car.

• You calculate distances between cities by how long it would take you by bike (*twenty-one bike days from St. Petersburg to St. Louis*).

• You know how many miles you rode last night, last week, last year.

• You don't find it oversharing to tell people you just met how many miles you rode last night, last week, last year.

• You have a Biker's Tan: the bottom two-thirds of your legs, the lower half of your arms, and two little circles on the tops of your hands.

• Your Biker's Tan scares small children at the public pool.

• You get sad when your Biker's Tan fades.

• You have nothing good to say about logging trucks or RVs with living fossils behind the wheel, or anything sporting wide mirrors.

• You have lost feeling in your hands, neck, and groin for substantial periods of time, but still you consider it the fair price of doing business on two wheels.

• You have far too many photos of yourself on or around your bicycle next to signs at the tops of mountain passes, WELCOME TO SO AND SO STATE, national park entrances, starting lines of bike rides, historic sites, and front doors of bicycle shops.

• You've lost sleep over the trailer-versus-pannier debate—of course you own both.

• You can't bring yourself to recycle any magazine remotely related to cycling (*Bicycling, Adventure Cyclist, Dirt Rag Bike,* even that issue of *GQ* where Al Gore was on a bike).

• You've given your bike a nickname.

• You've used that nickname out loud . . . in mixed company . . . and felt no shame or embarrassment. Some of us aren't so brave.

• You lift your butt off the car seat as you go over potholes, railroad tracks, and speed bumps.

• You turn the air vents of your car to blow directly into your face and imagine you are on a bike ride.

• You own a pile of lightweight stuff that has multiple uses, and you've tested all of them in real-life situations.

• You have enough funny/scary animals-chasing-me stories to close a bar of rowdy Irishmen or outlast a windbag uncle at the family reunion. (Note: No windbag uncle? Hmm, could be you.)

• You've slept in a church, playground, cemetery, farm pasture, yurt, and jail (voluntarily) beside your bicycle.

• You know the other definition of Critical Mass.

• You are an expert at spotting thunderstorms, tornadoes, windstorms, marauding cattle, and ice cream stands from a distance.

• You have been caught in a thunderstorm while still in the saddle blinking away water and grinning all the way home.

• You check your helmet mirror for what's behind you even when you are off the bike and not wearing it.

• You hate headwinds, hills, and trucks parked on the shoulder of any descent.

• You secretly love headwinds and hills, but those trucks parked on the shoulder of any descent are still the work of an angry god.

• You forget, much like a woman after childbirth, all the pain, headwinds, humidity, and hills within days of a long ride, and start dreaming about the next.

• You have cockroached: bonking so badly that you have to lie on your back, pull your arms and legs tight, and spasm your legs into the air to relive the cramps. Take a picture of that sometime.

• You can say "My bicycle has been stolen!" in six different languages.

• Your bike is more expensive than your car. (If you even own one.)

• You never ask anyone in a car if the road you are on has "hills" or "climbs."

• You wave to drivers with bike racks.

• You have convinced yourself and others that protein bars are tasty. Here, try the coffee, banana, peanut butter sundae ones. They're the best.

• You have tested your hypothermic limits and found that they can be expanded with pedal speed, layering, and hot cocoa.

• You agree with the statement: "If everything feels in control, you just aren't going fast enough."

Chapter 28

THE MORNING COMMUTE

I swear I don't look for trouble. I don't look for things to happen to me on a bike, but it seems that more often than not, when I pedal out the driveway, they do.

A couple of fellow bike travelers who have dog-eared copies of my books dropped me an email from south of the equator:

"Joe, we're halfway through Central America and not much has happened . . ."

My reply: "I pedaled downtown this morning with my boys and all hell broke loose."

Is it me? I haven't conducted a scientific study on why this is the case. No one seems willing to part with grant money for such an undertaking, and the fact that I'm not a trained scientist poses a . . . challenge, but if I had to hazard a guess, I'd say I'm a trouble magnet—good and bad—due to an uneven mix of things: my outgoing personality, a shoot-from-the-hip approach to problem solving, my lack of shame, and on account of being more spinal column than cerebral cortex.

Or I'm just one of those people. Take this morning's ride. I thought I was scheduled to appear on the local NBC affiliate morning show. Not owning a television is no excuse for misreading the producer's email. In my defense, "Pioneer Courthouse Square Studios at 6:45" could have meant a.m. or p.m. I've always done morning shows, not the evening news. Portland's come a long way in the bike world, baby, when I'm prime time. Often mistaken for homeless on wheels back in the day, now we're the active family feel-good segment at the end of the telecast. Or it's a slow news cycle.

In the cool of the predawn morning, I lit the bike up like a holiday tree and pedaled for downtown. When I say "the bike" I'm referring to the entire sixteen-foot mule-train setup—tandem, Trail-a-Bike, and trailer—which, after pedaling three thousand miles of Canada fully loaded, wasn't that hard to navigate without passengers or gear, but it did draw looks. I imagined myself the bicycle version of a school bus before the kids have loaded on for the day.It was peaceful at that hour, first light bathing Mount Hood in pink as I maneuvered over the Broadway bridge and arrived in the square to see a group of students, a band or chorus, holding a banner in front of the *Today*-show-style window. Teenagers are not easily impressed, but they turned in unison to have a look at my rig; smiles and gasps. I had a look at their poster and gave them the thumbs-up. We all looked into the window of the studio. Less excitement there, just green screens and a weatherman pointing around the solid-colored screen as if he were swatting mosquitoes. I took the hitch off the trailer to bring the rig into the studio. But my escort was nowhere to be found.

"I'm not sure what he told you, but I don't have you on the schedule." The network employee I raised by banging on the studio door was nice about it. When I mentioned which host I was to be chatting with, he offered a sympathetic smile.

"That's our evening news. I guess we'll see you back here in twelve hours."

Riding across the bridge for the second time in so many minutes, I noticed the sun was peeking between the buildings and the mountain now. Even though I'm not a morning person, it was a fine way to greet the day—a few hours earlier than I preferred, but my blood was flowing and I felt some color in my face, fully alive. Day or night, I'm never better than when I'm in the saddle.

"Hit 'em, hit 'em."

This from a brain trust behind the wheel of a truck whose size should be reserved for folks running ranches or mining operations in the Outback. He was waiting kitty-corner for the light as I took the right turn, and I suppose he was cheering on the car beside me to left-hook me into the next world. Classy. He made eye contact as he tossed out his twisted cheer, ending it with a loathsome little smile. Was he rooting for or egging on the car beside me?

The vast majority of drivers are accommodating, pleasant, and watchful, but when a guy like this affirms the stereotype you have to see it for what it is: someone who secretly hates his own choices, or is just plain evil. There is a meanness in this world and I ignore it at my peril.

But for pete's sake, I'm towing a Trail-a-Bike and a trailer. He's gotta see that there are kids in this equation. I'm projecting here, but his response might be something about cyclists not having a sense of humor. I don't confront . . . except to mouth the word "loser" as I round the turn and head for home.

Even if he didn't see me, that felt good.

I chanced a look back to see if he'd gone all Stephen King's *Chris-*

tine on me—jumping the light and hooking a U-turn to barrel down and finish the cheer himself—but it was far worse than that.

"Yikes!" I actually said the word *yikes* out loud.

I'd left the Trail-a-Bike and trailer detached and sitting out in front of the studio window. With the panniers and equipment inside the trailer, I calculated that I'd just left more than a thousand dollars' worth of gear in Portland's "living room" unattended.

As I pedaled back downtown, standing up and hammering the mule train à la the bell lap of a contested race, I wondered how long my possessions (some of the few possessions in this world I actually care about) would remain on display.

Twenty minutes is a lifetime to tempt people with unattended and unlocked goods in the big city. Perhaps the glee club or band members had watched over it in my absence. I wouldn't even care if they'd rifled through it for stuff, as long as the bulk of it was still there. Maybe the early-rising criminals would mistake it for a piece of art. There was always a chance the theft would be caught on the local news morning show. Cameras were rolling.

It's a good thing I didn't stop for that fortifying Snapple before turning around for my trailer. The security gal had already locked it up and called the police to take it to impound. I arrived at the same time as the cops. Another minute and my gear might have been swallowed up in red tape and hidden away like the boxed holy relic at the end of *Raiders of the Lost Ark*.

As I pedaled over the bridge . . . again, I felt fortunate that all the trouble—good and bad—I'd attracted had left me upright and enjoying the sunrise for the third time. Of course the day was still young . . .

Chapter 29

THE TRUTH ABOUT TUNNELS AND BRIDGES

Forget potholes, road rage, and rights-of-way.

Ask any saddle jockey what big-city obstacles send bursts of adrenaline and pangs of fear through the old central nervous system and it's always bridges and tunnels that top the list.

With bridges it's no shoulders, that big drop-off to the right, and grillwork surfaces that make one clench down on the handlebars and tighten up the sphincter. Tunnels are a different beast altogether—dark, claustrophobic wormholes where sounds roar about like a Class V rapid, then ricochet and Doppler off the walls until synapse-jamming noise is all one knows. Be it pedaling into Copper Canyon, Mexico, out of Auckland, New Zealand, or through Pittsburgh, Pennsylvania, there's always a dicey bridge to cross or deep, dank tunnel to gear down and burrow through.

Pittsburgh, my childhood home, has been called one of the most livable big cities in the country, but all those bridges and tunnels make entry to the Steel City tricky work for a cyclist. Rolling in for a homecoming, I resembled a spawning fish traveling on instinct. Fort Pitt Tunnel swept me in without time to consider the consequences. It went dark in a hurry, and a pair of Oakley sunglasses did not help matters. Allowing them to slip down the bridge of my nose was a mistake; I had to hold on to the handlebars and hope for the best.

Moments later, as I picked up speed, they dropped away like booster rockets. I think the sign instructed NO LANE CHANGING, but a guy on a cell phone behind the wheel of a BMW swerving inches from my frame obstructed part my view of it. He motored ahead without a nod or second thought . . . nice.

Fort Pitt Tunnel cuts right through Mount Washington, and some genius decided ceramic tiles were the way to decorate its interior. These square little merchants of death sporadically fall from the ceiling. I tried not to think about that as I took the lane and clicked into my highest gear. A quarter of the way through I had to make peace with the wartime-level noise, the eerie Space Mountain–style orange lighting, and the thick, choking traffic.

That's when the carbon monoxide hit me like a bag of wet dirt. I felt good in a really bad way—warm, spotty, and loose right down to my toes—it gives new meaning to the expression *light at the end of the tunnel*. I sprinted and squinted and searched for a patch of precious light, and just like that I was back out in the world . . . on a regal bridge with three rivers below and an awesome panoramic of a city I once knew and still loved. It would be so easy to forget those moments of terror in the hole. Before amnesia could set in, I vowed to find a better route out of town.

Another ride, another bridge, and I still hadn't learned much. Adhering to the Boy Scout code, I pride myself on being prepared. Failing that, and I often do, I drop back on the illusion of resourcefulness and an evolutionarily misguided lack of fear. Humility rarely enters the picture.

What can I say? I'm a cyclist and a journalist on top of that. A pompous combination that hammered the coffin shut on modesty years ago. I'll say this: Once Lycra is donned, humility can roar back to life at the first glimpse in a mirror, which I make a point to avoid.

I did manage to come face-to-face with plenty of humility during a windy day on the fringes of Copper Canyon, Mexico. It was a sag-supported bike tour—a writing junket I'd fallen into ass-backwards and was just happy to be aboard. The van checked on me before the lunch stop. I waved them by, thinking I was only a few miles from a quick bite and sit-down. Who needs a stinkin' van, anyway? Made it damn near 'round the world without backup, so why start going soft now?

There'd been a tailwind all morning, leaving me with strong legs and that stupid smile on my face. The one cyclists get when everything is rolling along. I had yet to notice the wooden suspension bridge. It appeared to be a thousand-foot drop to the valley floor.

What was I waiting for? Cars drove over it, but every time I rolled my wheels onto the wood I could see too much daylight between the slats. A decent wind didn't help matters.

The supreme insult arrived in the form of two elderly women and a child navigating their way toward me . . . a casual stroll over the gorge. The only thing worse would have been a gentleman sporting a walker shuffling over the wooden slats of doom. I waited, weak as a kitten. I could almost feel the testosterone leaving my body, but there was no way I was going to ride those slats.

Eventually, the van circled back. As I racked the bike and slid into the backseat, I comforted myself with the notion that I'm a twenty-first-century man, ambushed on occasion by the achievements of the nineteenth.

Chapter 30

THE NO-SHOULDER TREATMENT

The long and rocky road that leads to your door . . . From a seasoned biker's point of view, trust me when I tell you it's better to get the cold shoulder in this world than the no-shoulder treatment. No shoulder can mean pain. It definitely involves loose gravel, broken cement, glass, rocks of every color and creed, and the occasional old car part waiting to taco your wheel or make your tubes leak like an old guy after he's eaten a bag of those fat-free olestra potato chips someone forgot to recall. Frankly, I'd rather play a little one-on-one with Shaq, build a snow shelter gloveless halfway up Denali, or start the day trying to keep pace with the likes of Merckx, Armstrong, and LeMond. But log enough miles commuting, racing, or touring, and bailing into the ditch now and then is inevitable. Here's the Metal Cowboy's road-tested guide for surviving and thriving on the other side of the white line . . .

1. Logging trucks make the rules . . . period.

2. Squirrels and other rodents can be successfully negotiated at significant speeds. Armadillos, on the other hand . . . not so easy. And never, never brake into it. Absorb the bump of the carcass and

keep going.

3. Elderly and other RV drivers have absolutely no idea how far those oversized mirrors stick out. Don't let them test their geometry skills on you.

4. Avoid the temptation to slam on both brakes when bailing into gravel. Pump and stay steady or get ready to pick little stones out of your knees well beyond dusk around the campfire.

5. Just because a group of children along the side of the road wave, this does not exclude the possibility they are hiding rocks and other assorted projectile weapons. Look at their hands as you pull onto the shoulder.

6. Back to the RVs for a minute. A generous braking distance is always needed, and many drivers consider gravel and rocks off to the side or any relatively flat space to their left or right a perfectly acceptable bike lane.

7. Glass will only blow your tube if you show it fear, but Slime and Kevlar liners are the better part of valor when it comes to dry thorns and cactus stickers in the West.

8. Roadkill—squirrels, rabbits, snakes, cats, and the occasional raccoon carcass—can ruin a good ride. Dodge, duck, dip, and detour them whenever possible, and bunny-hop the rest.

9. When riding up or down long switchbacks with big drops off your right shoulder, it's best to just take the lane. No driver, even with a big engine, can take switchbacks very fast.

10. A roll is always better than a slide as long as you have the head and face protected. A slide is better than a head plant regardless of the circumstances. And a kiss is just a kiss unless you're unfortunate enough to be making out with the pavement. In these romantic sit-

uations you should always wear protection—not that protection—a helmet and gloves.

11. On a road bike anything more than a thirty-degree angle will probably bring you down. If the slope is steep and the gravel loose, I don't care how much time and money you've sunk into that baby, let the bike go. If it's tight pack or small weeds and brush then hold on, point the bike into the descent, and ride it out. While you're at it, try channeling some of those old *Fall Guy* episodes into your reactions. You can argue, but Lee Majors was really hitting his stride as an actor not to mention stuntman during that series.

Hey, it could be worse. You could be living and riding in the shoulderless, Mad Max style state of Florida for the rest of your days.

Chapter 31

LONG DIVISION

I was never very good at math . . . higher numbers just turned me angry in the same useless way that twelve hours of forcing the pedals into an unyielding headwind across, say, Arizona flatirons can cause a man to whimper and howl and question the state of the universe. Maybe that's why the only bike adventure I've ever turned tail and run from featured the word *divide* prominently in its name.

What's worse, I'd already kicked the spine of the Rockies where it hurt that old-man mountain range, when I went down in a stunned, and stunningly, bloodied defeat. It was reminiscent of a prizefighter who has the bout won, the opponent on the ring ropes, only to crumble to the mat off a wild punch from out of nowhere.

Winter—not just snowfall, flurries, or a crisp bite in the air, but the full force of a sustained arctic blast—ran me to ground. It was a seasonal change on the magnitude that divides those animals with fur from the ones that hibernate and those few endangered hairless fools on bicycles who, despite attempting to push north for one more futile, bone-jarring morning, are forced off the trail and into a pub to nurse mild frostbite, bruised knees and elbows, and a now ruined bike tour track record. I'm older, and some would argue weaker, but I can dig up only one theorem in the boneyard of long-forgotten middle school math tests that would have me complete those unfinished miles:

Question: What fuels the machine? Answer: Desire, desire, desire. They beat it into our heads back in school, didn't they? Show your work if you want credit for it. My work begins in Routt National Forest, Colorado, just above tree line, heading north . . . again, too late in the season.

Clearly I left a remainder hanging out there on the trail some years ago and it's time to even the equation. Sure, I'm tempting fate. The snow isn't here yet, but the frost is definitely on the pumpkins and it puts a bounce in my cadence and clarity to memories of warm laconic days, in the far south of my recent past. I was cruising the continental divide trail in northern New Mexico in late August when I came across this roundup at a little before noon.

Cattle moving with such force and steady power that I was glad the spin of the freewheel didn't spook them into turning all that trotting beef in my direction.

A real cowboy in a long coat atop a jet-black horse sent a slight nod my way. I felt as though I'd slipped into a TV commercial from the 1970s before they were told to stop advertising cancer sticks and bourbon during prime time.

I met up with the herd again close to dusk. This time I talked with one of those ranchers, and he told me to follow his lead if I wanted a bit of excitement. On the face of it, I know it was that seasoned fellow rounding up the animals, but the thrill of a cyclist helping corral heifers and bulls with a Bridgestone MB-5 mountain bike is a memory I hold dear.

Something else I learned that day . . . never complain to a real cowboy about time spent in "saddle." And so, as I race another winter to the Canadian border, up loose rock and down dry singletrack, I smile, not because it's clear that this time I'll make it—Vegas odds putting it at five-to-one against would be my guess—but sometimes you just know a thing needs to be seen through. Because win, lose, or draw, I've vowed never again to complain about any ride, anytime. Since the alternative is . . . not riding. Does it really matter whether everything evens out, and I end up with no remainder miles left for another day, as long as I get to keep trying to solve life's problems on a bicycle?

Call it new math, but using this type of division even a child could feel his way to the right answer . . . all he needs is two wheels and a bit of wanderlust.

Chapter 32

BEFORE MY S.U.B. BECAME A STATUS SYMBOL

The *New York Times* writes about Portland, Oregon, as if it were always a two-wheeled Oz, a place where cyclists, lost out in the urban wilderness, could simply click their clipless-shoed heels and be back at home in the saddle. But not so long ago it was just another town where biking your kids to school marked you as a freak, an outlier, a rogue.

I remember an SUV pulling even with our SUB (Sport Utility Bicycle) as both of us stopped at the light. Rain splashing furiously from the wipers as she brought the electric window down to say something.

"I'd like to help."

Well, now, I could have taken that as an existential query to the universe and replied with "Don't we all," but I suspected she was speaking to what she thought were my dire circumstances.

So I ask, who among us touring cyclists hasn't been mistaken for the homeless?

What with hauling our worldly possessions from town to town, putting our show on the road for weeks at a time . . . okay, maybe it hasn't happened to you. Perhaps your gear is always showroom-new, showering and shaving are regular parts of your routine, and the Lycra across your back has people thinking sponsorship rather than soup kitchen, but the rest of us, with that broken rain jacket zipper we've been meaning to fix, have pretended not to notice the faces of sympathy or disgust as we pedal along.

Only I wasn't on the road this time. I was rolling the streets of my hometown of Portland with my preschool-aged son, Quinn, in tow. If there is anywhere in America where a morning commute to preschool by bike wouldn't get a second glance? It's Portland. Portland today, that is. Eight years ago, I had the streets to myself. Not another family on bike in sight.

A few geeky businessmen on folding contraptions, a racer or two before breakfast, but I was the only daddy on two wheels. Owing to the career I've chosen, I don't maintain much of a dress code, and a writer who hasn't gone a week without shaving isn't trying hard enough. Besides, the pajama bottoms gave the appearance of plaid pants if you didn't look too hard. To make matters worse, that morning I was donating art supplies to the preschool. I had an easel sticking out the back of the Chariot trailer and various brushes and paint containers puffing up my panniers.

Quinn hadn't allowed me to remove the pool noodles or parade streamers from celebrations earlier in the year, so we were a pretty high-profile ride, a soggy float long after the party had ended; something of an eco-friendly refugee from a gay pride parade. She leaned out the window, heat blowing, radio playing classical music. I came closer, rain dripping off my helmet. I used my bike gloves to wipe my nose and swipe some hair out of my eyes, standard operating biker procedure whether one has a home or not.

"Which would help more, clothing or money?" I was so thrown by the question that I paused to let it compute. Was she asking if I needed charity? To a writer of some standing in this town? An author with his own bike rack in front of Powell's Books? A man in the process of hauling his own donations to his kid's school?

She shook her head, as if to dispel the insensitivity of her question. "I've offended you. Take both." She handed me the bag of clothes before I could react. There was a twenty-dollar bill on top. "I was dropping these at Goodwill, but maybe you could put them to use right now."

She was trying unsuccessfully not to stare at my pajama bottoms. The rubber band securing the right cuff was actually one of my wife's hair scrunchies. I tried to hand the bag back, but she was already pulling away.

"There are some really nice kids' clothes at the bottom," she yelled in retreat.

I protested but by then she was just taillights. And here I was thinking the five o'clock shadow thing was working, in a George Clooney kind of way. I had a good laugh with the other parents at the preschool. I was a little miffed that no one found the woman's actions outrageous.

One dad said, "See what happens when you ride that bike around loaded down for bear?" I nodded. "Yeah, what happens is your sons and daughter get to paint on an easel and there's an extra twenty bucks in the ice cream social fund."

In the years since, Portland's streets have filled with Xtracycles, bakfiets, Trail-a-Bikes, and trailers, to the point where a morning drop-off at the local school or a pickup at the end of the day boasts more SUBs than SUVs in the parking lot. No one's handed me cash or clothes in quite some time. I was an unkempt pioneer and proud to have laid the groundwork.

Still, I believe that were I to move to another part of the country today and roll out my SUB, I could be mistaken for homeless once more. I cheer for a time when it's so commonplace to see families on bikes, using them as transportation and gas-free vacations, that I'm pegged as just another fashion-impaired dad.

And for the record, hair scrunchies still work in a pinch.

Chapter 33

MY AIM IS TRUE, AND THAT HAT IS YOU

What sort of bicycle adventure writer would I be if I pulled up to my performances in a Lincoln town car with a driver at the wheel? A clean, rested, slightly drunk one would be the correct answer, but one lacking the street credibility and road warrior wisdom I like to exude, and what readers demand of world explorers.

Whenever possible, especially when I'm doing gigs in my backyard, the Pacific Northwest, I like to pedal to my book launches, stand-ups, and Irish Bard Style performances. It feels a bit like cheating to ride a bike on someone else's dime only to stand with a drink in hand and get paid to talk to people about myself for an hour or two. During college, I'd stand around with a drink in hand talking to people about myself, but all I got for my troubles was a hangover, a trip to the clinic, or both. Now they hand me a check. What a country!

But it's not the same without the bike ride on either end. To begin with, it's absurd and sublime, this act of promoting one's art, craft, labors—so I need the miles in the saddle to decompress and get right with myself. Not to mention it's too much fun. If you're not riding, you're not living.

In support of my second book I pedaled my way up to Seattle. The publisher was fronting hotels and meals and appearances at Third Place Books, Elliot Bay, and several suburban B&N's.

Due to faulty routing and timing issues, I was late. The timing problems were of my own making: I had calculated the time and distance it would take based on my previous ride between Portland To Seattle, when the interstate was shut down and I was drafting 5,000 of my friends and neighbors during the STP fundraiser ride. Also there was my need to explore a u-pick farm for peaches. This may have set me back another hour or two, but hmm boy . . . peaches. Needless to say, I was a bit bedraggled and shopworn rolling up to and through the lobby of that luxury hotel.

The desk clerk gave me a despicable little grimace and head shake when I wheeled a fully loaded touring bicycle up to the front desk. We had to go through the "get the manager. I'll wait" dance, but when they punched me up on their screen and saw I was booked in the top suite everyone made nice, the doorman even said something along the lines of "Very Good, Sir." as he wheeled the bike to some safe location.

The clerk, chipper and spry and playful now, mentioned that he needed to get a code clearance because another VIP had been mistakenly booked into my room earlier, but that it was all straightened out now. The idea that I was a VIP just proved the utter madness and lack of boundaries to this world.

I didn't give it another thought until I tossed down my panniers on the bed and noticed a distinctive hat on the end table near the door. At that moment there came a knock on my door. All I wanted to do was shower and center myself for the event that evening but I pulled myself up and answered the call.

Standing in front of me was Elvis Costello, in a fluffy white bathrobe, drinking a cup of tea. As if that wasn't enough, he did that thing he does when he squints and straightens his glasses.

"Hello, there was a dust up with the rooms earlier. I believe I left my hat in there."

I got him the famous hat and when he put it on I burst out laughing. He joined in.

"You should go on stage dressed like that tonight." I said. "I'd pay money to see it." Pause. "I'd pay money to see you anyway, except you went and scheduled a gig up against mine. It's not a good sign when the presenter would rather be at your gig than his own."

He told me if he had a dime for every time he'd rather be somewhere else than on stage . . . He asked me what I did, "Write stories that on the surface are about bicycle travel, but I'm really trying to illuminate the human condition through storytelling."

Elvis took a sip of his tea. "Same here, only I use a guitar over a bicycle."

It'd been almost twenty years and the other side of the continent since I'd showed incredible restraint with Tom Petty, and I wasn't about to make that mistake again. Jesus, I wanted to tell him that I'd burned the fucking vinyl down to the nub listening to My Aim Is True. That my first serious girlfriend was named Alison, sort of, so that when it ended I pedaled around singing it over and over, but adding a T. I wanted to tell him I could have held an entire conversation with him using just the lyrics of his songs. I wanted to ask him if he still had the desire to do the mystery dance.

Instead, we stood in the hallway between my suite and his bigger suite for another moment. "Right, then," He said. "Good luck."

As I pedaled to my gig, the sun setting across the Puget Sound, my rig loaded down with pounds of extra books and prizes and props, I wondered if I still had the desire to do my own little mystery dance. One good size hill stood between me and the venue. When I came out of the saddle wearing a shit-eating grin, pumping my legs and singing Costello songs at the top of my lungs, I had my answer.

Chapter 34

THE RAVIOLI RIDE

Everyone rides a bike in Italy: bankers in suits, bombshells in flowery dresses, old men carting baguettes and sausages back home in wire baskets. On the coast whole families pedal to the beach atop rusty clunkers, while in the hills you'll spot toothless nonas creeping up long hills, unfazed when packs of racers in tight Lycra blow by them.

It's mountain biking that's the last frontier in Italy. My brothers-in-law have a rich history of abusing me up the inclines and through rock gardens of Northern California's off-road landscape. When, last summer, a scheduled family reunion came together in northern Italy, I discovered that some of our Tuscan relatives were as nuts about mountain biking as their American counterparts.

I bet there's a gene responsible for this.

Of course, I was recruited for protection. My brothers-in-law always bring along someone they know will be sucking their air, mud, and rear wheels. What they didn't count on this time around? I've clocked some fairly brutal miles in the saddle since we last rode together. Two loaded tours across the continent hauling hundreds of pounds of children and gear. And while it wasn't off-road, it was over the spine of the Rockies. Most days I would have chewed my clipped-in feet out of a trap to do the steepest mountain bike climbs instead of the pack horse routine of pulling my wagon train over asphalt. Can you say rematch?

"Here's your bikes."

Phil and Rob, the brothers-in-law who think every ride is a race, scored the prized bikes from Gino and Perre Georgio. I was left with a no-name softtail contraption, but it seemed as if it would get the job done. Brad, my Buddhist brother-in-law, also signed on for the ride. I think his setup might have been a women's bike. As a new father, he wasn't in peak condition, either, but Brad has always been the wild card of the family. He flows like a river and lands on his feet.

Before we'd even taken to the saddles, everyone was sweating like businessmen in a hot sauna. Italy in June can be sweltering. It was this go-round.

We stopped by Gino's house to make a few adjustments to the rigs. Namely, mine. I'd discovered on the downhill to his farmhouse that the handlebars were so loose that it was only the amount of time I've lived on a bike, a child-like defiance of gravity, and finally grabbing the front stem below the bars that kept me from crashing. While at Gino's, Phil discovered that his sweet rig had some gearing issues and the shocks had seen better days. Karma, baby.

We roared down into the valley where the walled city of Lucca lies, but as if following an army in retreat, just as quickly we swung to the right before reaching its outskirts, then settled in for a breathless climb up into the mountains. Gino explained that these forested peaks allowed many to elude the Germans during World War II. Women and children, comfortable walking the hills daily on their olive-harvesting routes, took to the high country before the enemy could catch its breath. As the winding roads became cartoon steep, I pretended I was a peasant woman pulling a load of olives behind me.

It might have helped a little.

Our ride took us through little villages sporting ancient churches, little restaurants, and statues of saints hidden among the flowering plants and lush canopies.

My bike took me to the ground not once, but twice. Each time the back wheel came out from behind me on some fairly easy gravel downhill. It was over-inflated. I had a few cuts and would probably be sore the next day but I was relatively unscathed by the time we deflated the problem. I stayed upright the rest of the ride.

The tree cover that shaded the roads and trails was our only salvation. When we'd pull back into the open sun, the temperature would jump ten degrees. I was the butt of early razzing due to the fact that I'd brought along maybe two gallons of tea and water to the rest of the crew's two water bottles. That and I'd packed about half of the twelve-course, catered dinner buffet we'd all enjoyed the previous night. Let them laugh. My entire load weighed less than my two-year-old when he was being towed across Canada.

I snacked at every stop while hydrating *and* showering on the move.

Halfway up the mountain we arrived at a king's estate. Not just kingly for its size but actual royalty. It was something out of a storybook. The scope and detail of the buildings and grounds put Europe's age and historical significance into some perspective. It was also the first time my relatives gained some perspective on the amount of food and water calories they'd been burning up the mountain. Phil commented on how good those baguette pizza appetizers had been. This, as I popped another one out of my pack, looked directly at him, then swallowed it whole.

Another three miles of brutal climbing was rewarded with a spring-fed well. As I hoarded another slab of grub, my helmet fell into a stagnant pool of holding water.

Again, karma, baby.

After that, I asked my brothers-in-law if they wanted any of my food supplies. They did; pride had left the trail with the spike in temps and angle of elevation. Waves of fragrances washed over us. The hillsides were raging with flowers in full bloom. It hit me also that ours were the only bike tracks on these trails. As if someone had moved the best singletrack riding on the West Coast of America to a place no crowds could reach. A magical ride even in a hundred-degree heat.

Gino and Georgio both wore their bike shorts rolled up to expose their thighs. I thought perhaps it was another of those crazy fashion trends the Italians are famous for starting. If it were, I hoped it wouldn't come to America anytime soon.

"We wear them like this to tan as much skin as possible," Gino explained. "If construction workers could wear Speedos in Italy, they would."

This was not an exaggeration. It's the only part of the world where I've seen a highway flagger wearing a reflective vest but no shirt as he waved cars through.

Then we were on top. The view afforded us a glimpse of the ocean, Pisa's tourist mecca, and the Italian Alps to the north. As we admired and snapped photos, far below, in one of the small villages we'd pedaled through, a choir of voices could be heard. They were singing ethereal songs in the morning sun, like the people of Whoville from the Dr. Seuss story.

"They're practicing for the Festival of the Holy Ravioli," Georgio noted. "It's actually for a saint, but if you've ever tasted the food served at the festival, you'd know exactly what they're singing about."

"Can anyone go?" I asked.

"Anyone who can stay up late. All our summer festivals are held at night."

I thought about a midnight snack, raviolis perhaps, all the way down the mountain.

Chapter 35

ALONG FOR THE RIDE

There are times we live for somebody else. This was not one of those times. Bolzano, Italy, is what happens when a German Fraulein and a boisterous Italian soccer fan get together and move to the mountains.

I'm here to ride bicycles, to take in the air, culture, people . . . but mostly to ride bicycles. There's a story to be written about the region and the bicycle touring company, Ciclismo Classico, pampering me across northern Italy for the better part of two weeks. And after a full year of being a cargo biking dad, I'm here so I'll be a better, fully functioning father to my four sons upon my return.

My cab ride from the train station to the hotel got things started with a bang. Normally, I'd move directly from plane to bicycle to explore a country, but being at the scheduling and bike equipment mercy of the touring company, I'm staying one night at a randomly selected place found on the Internet, owing to jet lag and its inscrutable name, The Business Resort Park Hotel Werth.

The female cabbie—an angry hybrid of fashion and fierce facial expressions—argued with me from the word go. I leaned in the passenger-side window and asked if she knew of the hotel. She kept looking at me as if I were asking her to get me on the last copter out during the fall of Saigon.

She kept yelling "Which one?" And I mean yelling the way you would tell your child not to touch the stove. "Which one? There are two. Which one?"

I spelled out the whole name, but she only seemed interested in the Werth part. She didn't like that I was adding an *r* to the name. So I spelled it a third time without the *r*. She offered a curt nod and told me to get in.

Tossing my pack across the backseat, I noticed for the first time that I was in the cleanest cab in the known world. She looked appalled. My backpack, my general appearance, the smell of a man who has several thousand miles of traveling on planes, trains, and buses between showers.

Again with the yelling. "Careful!" she barked, looking at my pack as if it were an insect.

This happened as I was saying, "Excusi." But for what I didn't know. The pack was soft and damaged nothing. She drove in the wrong lanes. I mentioned that the weather was perfect, just the way I like.

She looked at me like I needed to be fed to a lion. Her dismissive glance in the rearview said, *Your likes and dislikes are no concern to me, lion meat.* We turned down an alley. At this point, either I would be killed by her gang of nihilists who would also be holding The Dude's rug, or this was the super-secret back way to the hotel. It was the super-secret back way to the hotel.

She announced, "You. Here." But her expression was more, *We've arrived and you did not kill me or vice versa, so win–win.* I saw the spelling of *Werth* in fact has an *r* in it. In a nod to abusive relationships, I tipped her heavily.

She looked stunned. We both knew that she had been, how you say? abrupt.

"That could be for the smile you'll give the next tourist in your cab?" I asked as I let the money go. The smile she offered still had a bit of fang to it. She barked, "Addio!" as I made sure my pack did not disturb any part of the vehicle on the way out. My own smile was way too large heading into the reception area of Business Resort Park Hotel Werth.

I live for the moment on a trip when things shift and you go from being a tourist to a traveler.

Chapter 36

THE BEER
IN BOLZANO

The Business Resort Hotel Park Werth was a universe unto itself.

After parting with my curt cabbie, I enter a world in which the German owner is, like all women at work in Italy, dressed to the hilt. She has slicked-back jet-black cropped hair, a crisply starched white dress, and a tan that speaks of dermatology appointments in later years.

She is as pleasant as the cabbie was taciturn, but I don't learn this for some time. She is busy discussing tomorrow's breakfast with her friend or a staff member or someone more important than an American tourist.

So I wait on the step of an ornate lobby with the establishment's monstrous German shepherd. I speak with the dog. But I am no whisperer, meaning he looks at me with what could be friendship or *I will attack if you put that jet-lagged sweaty paw any closer.* I have been wrong about dogs before. That's when he rolls over on his back and I give him a pet and a scratch. We're simpatico.

It's from this vantage point I notice a small fleet of upright handlebar bikes that look to have been sent over from the set of Il Postino. I must ask if they are for use or rent or what not.

Now she's ready for me, but it doesn't matter. I don't speak more than a few words of German, Hogan's Heroes German I call it, and her English is a parlor trick. She says words in English that seem to make sense, but the results do not match. "It's has air-conditioning . . . it's good." *It* meaning "the room," and despite her words, it did not.

But I was too tired for a linguistic shadow boxing match and the breakfast sounded amazing so I figured I'd crack the window and hope for the best. I went in the pool to wake up. This is a trick I learned when traveling. If you stay awake until the sun goes down, no matter where you started the day, you can fool your body into the new time zone.

The German tourist couple sitting out on the pool lounge chairs laughed and said I was crazy. "Too cold!" They must be from the surface-of-the-sun part of Germany.

Yes, I may borrow one of the Il Postino bicycles. I was also given directions to several eateries by my host. Alas, her directions in English were perhaps to another village or an alternate universe. Either way, I stumbled upon a real gem while looking for something else. Cheese tortellini with artichokes, a salad to die for, Forst beer, and a bar full of raging soccer fans. The best time, if not the safest biking I've ever done in my life, to roam around an unfamiliar town is when you are so jet-lagged that you feel slightly drunk before the first beer.

Comfortably numb I believe it's called. I ate outside, eyeing the steep cliffs around Bolzano and enjoying the fervor of the soccer fans, when a hornet the size of a baseball—this thing was a real horror show—began circling my table, looking to land on either me or my bright-gold beer. I'd downed more than half of it, but there was enough left to attract this killer insect . . . I don't usually worry over bees buzzing around meals—but this thing was some sort of genetically modified monster, a creature-feature matinee prop—it had trouble not tipping the sturdy pint glass over but it managed to land on my rim and went in for the beverage. My waitress took this as a cue to casually cover the top with a newspaper and shake the hornet fiercely but casually into the liquid. We watched the beer coat over and kill the beast.

"It's quite large, no?" I asked. She shrugged. "Ma." It was the size of a small pigeon.

Now I was frightened of anything around Bolzano with wings. Every bug or slightest noise near my ear during the bike ride back caused me to jerk and weave and wave my head around; Il Postino, the Epilepsy Edition. She brought out another full beer. I begged off, but she set it in front of me, gave me the famous Italian shoulder shrug—the same one I've seen my wife give me so often—and an accompanying look that said, *American, pleeassse!,* and nodded over at the big screen showing the World Cup to indicate this was a national holiday of sorts. Anyone not drinking was suspect.

So I drank and got out of there before anyone put another mug in my hand. Retracing my pedal over as best I could, jerking and head bobbing my way back to my hotel room as the crescendos of cheers from rabid World Cup fans poured down from apartment buildings and roadside pubs. And everywhere Italian flags and sheets and banners displayed the nation's colors.

I woke up with a start at 2 a.m. bathed in a sweat so thick I had to shower in cold water until I lost my breath, then slept with a washcloth on my forehead. I felt like I was dying. I took the window off its hinges, thinking how I'd explain that in German.

It cooled down a little. Nothing more than a hot room and jet lag . . . but I didn't see how I'd ever find the strength again to ride a bicycle. In the morning I was fit as a fiddle. The owner came out dressed in a full-on Bavarian tavern waitress outfit, which completely made up for the sauna of a room. And breakfast tasted even better than what they'd been conspiring over when I had to wait with the big dog the afternoon before.

Danke schoen.

Chapter 37

FIVE-STAR BIKE TOURING

I meet my fellow cyclists over caprese salad and cheeses of the region at a luxurious spa in Glorenza. After the meet-and-greet lunch we're introduced to our carbon-fiber Bianchis. The plan involves knocking out a warm-up ride to the towns around Glorenza—Clusio, Laudes, Malles—before dinner on the veranda. "The valley is wide and open, the air clean with the scent of flowers, and there are fantastic views of the Ortles mountain to the south and Monte Maria's abbey to the north."

But what the brochure doesn't mention is the screaming hill right out of the driveway and into the first town—which was holding its annual tractor festival. As we pedal east of town, a parade of colorful tractors doing ten miles per hour en route meets our parade of bicycles.

One of our guides, Marcello Bonini, a former racer and someone comfortable in the world, both in and out of the saddle, catches up to me. I've outpaced the group, not because I'm trying to be cocky, but because they've put me on a six-thousand-dollar bike with no extra weight to carry along the newly resurfaced roads at the borders of Italy, Switzerland, and Austria. I'm like a servant (who normally carries 150 pounds of human cargo and another 75 pounds of stuff) released from indenture. I could not feel lighter or more nimble if I tried.

We have a conversation about the absurdity of too much comfort and the merits of ending some days in this life cold, wet, tired, bloody, and exhausted.

"But that's not what's in store for you this week," he says. "If you like though I'll try my best to beat you up with extra miles."

We pedal along and I realize that I should just embrace the luxuries of the moment. When in Rome (or close to it) and all that… I can always sleep outside without my tent on the next adventure. I make a promise, as I glide on the carbon fiber wings of that bicycle, to do a long ride next fall without enough of everything as penance. But about those extra miles, yes please!

"Hey," Marcello says. "If you want to cross over to Switzerland, it's just five kilometers up this road. You'll be back before the rest of the group catches this turn."

"Do I need my passport?"

Marcello grins. "Only if the cows want to see it. If you don't blink you'll see a marker showing you've crossed over."

Chapter 38

ITALIAN FOR NEANDERTHALS

Our guide Jessica said that the Bio-pool at Hotel Rossl was to die for. It was a man-made body of water that used plant life to keep it clean, which I think we used to call . . . a lake. At any rate, I swam in it, and also the traditional pool on the other side of the hedgerow, as well as the indoor pool just for good measure, because it was there, because the only thing better than sleep at the end of a good day of cycling is swimming away strained muscles, and I love pulling a hat trick no matter the sport.

But it was the lake I couldn't get enough of. I climbed out of bed, slipped into the cool fresh water, and enjoyed a sunrise with kestrels and finches dropping in and out for morning drinks. Jessica was right.

That day we had a long and lovely climb up to the mountain village of St. Paul. The closest rider was a half mile back when I stood and danced on the pedals. If a cyclist dances on the pedals in a forest of olive trees and country road up a Cat 2 climb and there's no one there to see him doing it, does he still make a sound? Hell yes, he does. And for the record it sounds like heavy breathing and desire.

I reached the community fountain in the center of town. I dunked my head and waited in peaceful silence for the rest of the group.

At this hotel, I discovered that if you took the stairs up to your room instead of the elevator, you would be rewarded with a selection of croissants and apples at each landing. Ah Italy . . . you know my deepest desires, so well.

We took some time out of the saddle to breathe in high mountain air and hike around Oberbozen, Soprabolzano. A quick, spacious tram ride that gave us a bird's-eye view of pinnacles and terraced agriculture then put us in *Sound of Music* country. From there we hiked into the forest and around a lake. It's said that this is where Freud came up with his most lasting ideas. I, on the other hand, made a few whimsical observations and saw a dragon and a whale pattern in the clouds.

From there, Marcello and Jessica led us to the amazing Bee Museum, where they actually used a bike chain/ring system atop a barrel to separate the honey from the cone slabs without destroying the combs. From there our guides fed us cake and hiked us up to a llama farm. It was a climb for some of the folks in need of a bit more rest on rest day, but our trusted guide Marcello sang a medley of songs and kept everyone laughing.

Having spent a week wandering around backcountry New Mexico on assignment with a llama trek, I can tell you these animals, while regal and excellent hat and sweater providers, are not to be trusted. And true to form, after lunch, when I went to meet the champion llama, several of his pals were having relations in the pen across the barn. This brought quite a bit of laughter to the girls who were attending horse riding summer camp, and looks of horror from other llama farm visitors who ran over to the pen, thinking perhaps the loud noises were how llamas greeted people or something other than nature in all its glory.

Back in Bolzano we took in the absolutely fascinating tour of the five-thousand-year-old man discovered in a nearby glacier. As I stood in front of the window housing the discovery, kept cool in a climate-controlled room, Marcello put his hand on my shoulder.

"Neanderthal, meet Neanderthal."

Chapter 39

GIFT OF THE TYROLEAN MAGI

There is little to no hope for me in the fashion department, which in itself creates, shall we say, its own style category. Still, there's every reason on a supported group bicycle tour to maintain a basic level of hygiene, even when wearing a green dry-fit shirt with, say, a red pair of socks sporting images of Bigfoot on them. At least from the neck up you can look like you belong indoors.

I was too rushed before the adventure to get my summer haircut. Instead, I'm sporting something wild and unkempt that, with or without the proper tools, can quickly move from crooner Chris Isaak's famed pompadour to Bill the Cat territory.

My resourceful guide is no help in this area. Being a swimmer and a man with some foresight, Marcello has chosen a short cut that needs no comb.

No one in the group has a comb, either, at least no one is offering one up for me to share, no stores have one for sale each day, nothing . . . I go five days finger-combing this thicket to comical result. Front desk after front desk in top-flight hotels, because of either a gap in communication or some failure on my part—I've never been good at the game Charades—is unresponsive to my comb requests.

Then I meet a vision of loveliness behind another front desk. She is at least six feet tall, decked out in her *Sound of Music* traditional dress; it would appear that Heidi has returned from the mountains to aid in my search. After much back-and-forth her eyes light up. I hear her repeating the word *comb* to herself like a benediction as she heads into a back room. She is gone for a while. Perhaps she is making me a comb? When she returns she hands me a work of art: It is handmade, a beautiful selection of several different types of woods. This would be the nicest hair-care product I've ever owned. I ask if I can take this treasure to the bathroom if I promise to return it, or should I just try to make something presentable of my bird's nest right here in the lobby?

She looks at me with the intensity of a tall, blond, angular species from a faraway place trying to make friendly, peaceful contact with a frightful-looking alien from a world where hair care has gone wanting . . . "You take. You keep." Translation: *No one wants that comb back after it touches your head.*

And I have nothing to give in return. So I offer her a smile and an awkward half bow, and realize that I had become, for a few moments, Bill Murray in *Lost in Translation.*

Chapter 40

SURRENDER, SURRENDER, BUT DON'T GIVE YOURSELF AWAY

A classic cycling gear moment came after lunch on the fifth day of my tour through northern Italy. I was informed that there were bargain-basement prices on bicycle jerseys in the square.

Sure enough, a complete race team was feasting over these awesome bargains when I arrived. I conversed with them in my broken Italian and felt a bit like Davy in the film *Breaking Away* . . . until I tried on the largest of the jerseys and it fit over one biceps . . . cosi, cosi . . . but you can't have it all.

On the off chance there is a traditional heaven, and it does not offer up riding, friendships, views, and tasty croissants the size of catcher's mitts filled with cream, apricots, or apples, I will have no choice but to ask the deity in charge to kindly return me to northern Italy and Ciclismo Classico.

One heavenly experience that was quite unexpected and surreal involved climbing legend Reinhold Messner. Growing up on stories in outdoor magazines (which I would go on to write for) of daring and adventure and risk, I have long known of Messner. In the climbing world there is no one more epic, for his accomplishments—the first to summit Everest without supplemental oxygen—and for the way he has conducted himself as a person. Imagine if talent-wise, Michael Jordan, Arthur Ashe, and the Beatles occupied one skin. And used that skin to top all of the world's peaks. Then tried to make the world a better place once they returned to sea level. This is who Messner is to the alpine world and beyond. Marcello, an unsung renaissance man in his own right, afforded me the opportunity to talk to and get a photo with Messner. The bike tour included a lunch at Messner's Castle/Museum, which sits high up in the hills above Bolzano. It was a picture-perfect afternoon. I'd met a god of the climbing world in his castle, but what really completed the day had nothing to do with Messner but a conversation I had with Marcello. He was driving the van that day. Having run a bicycle touring company myself, I know that van driving day can be brutal when the pedaling everyone else is getting to is so sweet . . . but at each stop we'd be treated to a variety of music, from jazz to Italian polkas to Cheap Trick—which, Marcello and myself being nearly the same age, we discussed in a larger conversation about first concerts. Marcello sang along to everything . . . and unlike my voice, his is beautiful. It's not an exaggeration to say it's what a sweet soul dream sounds like.

Nevertheless, he put up with me attempting to harmonize with him on "Surrender, Surrender, But Don't Give Yourself Away." I was a good twenty minutes ahead of the groups so we talked, just the two of us, some more and I discovered that we'd both pursued active lives and a love of bicycles, both laughed at the sublime and absurd in our days, both seen some incredible musicians live, and both married tall, lovely Tuscan women.

I was quick to point out that I had done all of this without his looks and fashion sense so, really, who was the real magician between us?

But what endeared Marcello to me beyond measure was the point in the tour when another guest pointed out—and it was not said with guile or maliciousness, just a privileged cluelessness—that with Marcello's skills, his endless talent, it seemed he could be making so much more money. Marcello just smiled in his open, inviting way and said, "You know, my friend, the pawn and the king go into the same box at the end of the game."

Surrender, surrender,
But don't give yourself awwwaaaayyy!

Chapter 41

FED TO THE LIONS

This was no disco . . . this was the Opera Aida in the Verona Arena with rainstorms building just as the players took the stage. We had our candles lit and the arena was twinkling from top to bottom; then the lightning crashed and the drops turned into rain. Unlike sporting events where everything plays on, the expensive musical instruments cannot handle even a light shower.

I used my Arkel backpack as a rain cover, and lent my new friend Haley, working as a nanny in Italy for the summer, the plastic bag the pillow came in as a rain jacket. Then it stopped and we waited, ever hopeful, and bought Fantas as they swept water from the stage.

When it started up for the second time with lightning frighteningly close, we all scurried into the catacombs of the interior of the arena. No one was leaving yet—not at these prices—no one.

I had the feeling of being an unlucky Christian about to be released into the lions' den, with only a backpack and a hotel pillow I'd smuggled in to sit on for weapons. I suppose I could have tried to smother the beast or sell it on the durability and many other features of an Arkel product. Instead of gladiators, though, there were fashionable women, many of them Italian, but from all across Europe, and all dressed to kill. Most were violating the no-smoking-in-the-catacombs policy announced often and loudly over the speakers.

Each time it would repeat in three languages, these femme fatales would offer a tight smile and a shoulder shrug, then continue smoking. I decided that were we to face lions in the rain tonight, I would stand behind several of these gorgeous, deadly creatures as they used their stilettos, diamond-encrusted lighters, and withering glances to cut a path to safety.

Then the clouds lifted, the last light left the sky, the shop-vacs sucked up any stage water, and the show began. It was an amazing evening. The sets were strange, elaborate, and captivating. The costumes a bit like *Battlestar Galactica* meets Cleopatra, and the music, the voices. The story, what I could glean of it, was about love found, paraded, battled over, stopped and ended together, buried alive in a tomb . . . a playful romp really in which the trapped lovers went out singing with their last breath.

Not a bad way to wrap it up. "Always look on the bright side of death . . . now, just the gentiles."

But what amazed me most was how the opera singers performed without microphones or any additional amplification, yet still you could hear them clearly from anywhere in the arena because of the way the building was designed . . . and they were talented as fuck-all.

With the rain delay of forty-five minutes and three twenty-minute intermissions, the show ended at 2:15 a.m. Finding our hotel shuttle bus among three hundred other hotel shuttle buses was a whole other adventure. People were left behind, I witnessed this, but all's fair in love, war, and opera.

Sometimes you get lucky. I spent the day roaming the streets of Verona by rental bike far and wide, with a good book in hand and a bright-yellow umbrella in my pannier, just in case it rained or a curious monkey wanted to find me—I don't wear hats, yellow or otherwise. My last stop was the Cathedral of Zeno. The rain hit while I was inside so I found some amazing art including one that looked a bit like a Dalí—it had real nails sunk into the paint all over the canvas. Made the short walk back to my hotel with gelato in one hand and my yellow umbrella at full sail. I will miss many things about Italy, but my waistline will not miss a gelato stand literally every twenty feet.

Here's what a brain trust I am. For my entire stay in Italy I used the stairs in all the posh hotels, mostly to justify the croissant intake. At each landing I'd see PIANO 1, PIANO 2, and so on. I thought, *How civilized, they have a piano on every floor.* Granted, I heard no piano, and paying all the musicians in a five-story hotel could get a little spendy; why not just use the piano in the lobby downstairs? *But wow, it must be a thing in high-class hotels . . . the Italians really know how to live, with a piano bar on every level . . .*

On my last day in-country, as I followed a women's synchronized swimming team from Switzerland (I kid you not) up the stairs, it finally hit me: There's no basement in the Alamo, and *piano* means "plane" or "level" in Italian. I acknowledged this out loud with a boisterous "Of course!" that reverberated through the stairwell and startled, if not frightened, many members of the swim team. There was much whispering in Swiss/German, and no eye contact. My work was done here.

As the sun set, figuratively and literally, on my Italian Bike Adventure with Ciclismo Classico, I was given a final take-your-breathaway evening. Even this little village a mere kilometer from the airport was wrenchingly picturesque. Looking at a shot from the hotel room window, then thinking about views from those Holiday Inn Express locales near any airport back home . . . no contest. There was something incredibly soothing about watching a nature program in German with a Windham Hill sampler soundtrack in a hotel room in Italy.

I was trying to get some writing done in my room when the nature program ended and MTV Classico started up with something called *Estate 1987*—100 percent classic hits and misses.

Holy crikey . . . never had there been a more absurd and sublime archive of pastel clothing, walls of hair, speedboats being improperly steered by musicians, bored models standing around completely dry at swimming pool parties (that hasn't changed), and castles overlit by zillions of candles, always featuring robed, clearly professionally trained dancing monks, the sound of synthesizers everywhere, and Madonna in an oversized suit she must have rolled David Byrne to acquire.

Samantha Fox, Pet Shop Boys, Phil Collins, the Blow Monkeys, Huey Lewis demonstrating "The Power of Love," and George Michaels desperately trying to convince everyone that he wants your sex, ladies . . . and then out of left field he offered up a PSA, written in lipstick on a thigh no less, about exploring monogamy . . . All fun and games until Whitney Houston came on . . . she was so young and bubbly and her voice was like butter and she just wanted to dance with somebody . . . somebody who loved her. Not long after this was made she found Bobby Brown. I see her in my mind's eye drifting away alone in that hotel bathtub. Be careful what you wish for.

I couldn't believe I was tearing up over MTV Classico *Estate 1987*.

This never happened when I traveled the world as a single man, but now that I had a family, I had a stake in this world outside of my-self . . .

Then Everything but the Girl's "I Miss You Like the Deserts Miss the Rain" to wreck me completely. It was one of the songs I wore out between meeting Beth and getting together for good.

So on one hand, Italian MTV taught us that we have to be careful what we wish for, but on the other, the heart wants what it wants . . . I can't say I was careful over the miles in the saddle, just lucky I guess.

And when I fell down, I always found a way and a reason to get back up.

Chapter 42

THE BITTER END

My mother never learned how to ride a bicycle. She was about ten years old when she took a tumble trying to learn on one during a holiday in Spain.

That was sixty-five years ago. I've been threatening to take her on a ride since 1987, but with her arthritis I've always needed something more secure than the back of my cargo bike.

Then came the fall in her apartment, the long night and part of the next morning when she was unconscious, days in the hospital when we didn't know if she'd make it, the rehab. But she's a tough old bird and she was ready to come home. She did come home.

Then they found the cancer.

And that's when I found a Pedicab bicycle. When I explained the situation to my friend, he told me I could use it on short notice whenever she was ready. She smiled when I told her the plan.

"You know, through your books I feel like I've always been right there with you every mile. But whenever you want to take me for a real ride, I'm ready."

Weeks went by and the weather wouldn't cooperate. We tried to keep things as they'd always been, Sunday-night dinners at my place.

The revelations all come tumbling out after Mom asks Sawyer to teach her some of his favorite songs. All things considered, she's doing quite well, for someone with lung and colon cancer—frail, "little uncomfortable at times" is the most we get out of her regarding pain, but able to travel to my house, eat, laugh, and enjoy! I position her as the queen of the house on my big purple love seat with lots of pillows and a TV tray for some of Beth's special Sunday-evening sauce and fresh-made pasta.

Sawyer wants to do all the verses of "Michael Row the Boat Ashore" so I Google it. When we're done singing, I point out that it was a Peter, Paul, and Mary song.

"Mary was always nice to me when they'd sit and drink with us at The Bitter End."

The room is silent. Mom looks up from her pasta. "What?"

I am nonplussed. And for those who know me, this is a very hard state to put me in. When I regain my voice I say,

"Mom, are you saying you hung out with Peter, Paul, and Mary at The Bitter End in Greenwich Village—also called America's Nightclub and personified in the film *Inside Llewyn Davis*?"

"Sure. It was around the corner from our apartment. We were young and broke so it was something to do."

I'm literally staggering about the room now. It's not every day that you learn that your parents were beatnik folkies.

"Woody Allen would play his clarinet and tell jokes. Dad told him to stick with the music."

"So you were regulars?"

"Oh, yes. We started going right after it opened in '61 and went all the time until we moved in '63."

"Who else do you remember seeing?"

Mom, setting down her silverware, realizing that she has an audience now.

"Sometimes four or five musicians a night. Lots of comics and some people reading poetry. Miles Davis. And Flip Wilson was really good. Dad was always chatting and laughing with Lenny, but I thought he had a potty mouth."

Lenny fuckin' Bruce?

"Jesus Christ, Mama . . . just . . . Jesus . . ."

"Well, it was just around the corner and free."

She goes on to tell us about Van Morrison kicking over tables, and the time Dad, often in his fisherman sweater and with a beautiful baritone voice of his own, got up on stage to do harmonies with either the Everly Brothers or the Isley Brothers. Mom isn't quite sure.

"George Carlin was what Dad called good rude."

At this point my head explodes.

"But Joan Rivers had them all beat."

My pasta has gone cold but I can't stop shaking my head.

"Cass Elliot was another one I really liked. She was good by herself and with the Mamas and the Papas. Everyone loved Bob Dylan but I was more of a Bill Haley fan. I know we were there when Peter, Paul, and Mary recorded a concert at the club."

Then it all came back to me. The afternoons in Pittsburgh dancing around the living room to Irish Rover records while my Dad sat in calm repose in his fisherman's sweater smoking cigarettes as I thumbed through records by Joan Baez, Richie Havens, the Kingston Trio, and John Lee Hooker. On the slip cover of an Irish Rovers album, I recall a bunch of names written in marker.

"Oh yes, Dad always kept lists. Those were likely all the folks we saw at the club. But it didn't include anyone from when we went to see Chuck Berry play over at The Cotton Club. He'd been so good at The Bitter End."

My dentist fixed Mom's smile. She was so thrilled to be able to smile again without covering her mouth with her hand, and when I brought her back for a teeth cleaning she said it felt really good. I had to engage in a bittersweet conversation with my dentist about her cancer and what future procedures made sense and which didn't.

It was tough not to tear up in the waiting room.

The cancer specialists have given us several options, none of them worth a damn. I'm amazed at my mom's grace and strength in turning it all down.

This is to be her Indian Summer.

After the dentist's, we I steer the Pedicab down to the riverfront. When I look back she's got her eyes closed, the sun on her face; her beret is the epitome of Portlandia cool. I park in the shade and climb into the back so I can seat with her on the bench seat. I unwrap some sandwiches. She's not very hungry so we hold hands in comfortable silence. The Pedicab has a sound system built under the bench.

"Is this Paul Simon? I like him."

Mom asks me to take off the pickles. A young mother pushing a stroller walks by; she has maybe ten tattoos.

"So many people have tattoos," Mom notes. "Only sailors got them when I was raising you guys." She smiles over and I can see the face of the young lithe dancer she once was.

She folds the sandwich paper. It reminds me of leaving the bakery with her before I was old enough to join my sister in school yet. She would get me a gingerbread man cookie with raisin eyes, And when I'd look up she would fold the little paper in the same way she's folding the sandwich wrapper now.

"Did you ever want a tattoo?" she asks.

I nod. "Couple times but then the mirror would look back at me and say, 'Don't you dare fuck with this masterpiece.'"

No matter the time, place, or situation I kid and poke fun with my mom. It's always been this way. I guess I just love making her laugh.

Her new smile really does look nice. She squeezes my hand.

"So we'll have a few more laughs before I go."

I nod.

"That how I want it," she says.

"And maybe I'd better get that tattoo."

We shake the cab with our laughter.

Hard times? I'm used to them
The speeding planet burns, I'm used to that
My life's so common it disappears
And sometimes even music, cannot substitute for tears

David

Touched base with the neighborhood Fisher King tonight. We stood together in front of the library. He wanted to schedule a bike lockup this week so he can keep taking care of himself. I asked him if there was anything else, specifically, he needed. He has really kind eyes, you get to see them when he makes contact. This time he looked directly at me. "No . . . I'm really happy these days . . . pretty happy. What you've done, and gotten others to . . . I want to say . . . thanks." I thought he was finished, but he added, "And never asking me how I got here."

I nodded. "We're all just here, eh?" He patted his bicycle, gave me a smile, and pushed into the night. I gripped my handlebars and did the same. He went it alone, and I was headed back into the arms of my family.

I'm not gonna bullshit anyone. I've never gotten comfortable with the knowledge that I will die. It hasn't stopped me from living the hell out of this life, taking my moments, but that smug bastard is always in the audience, waiting, patient, nonnegotiable . . . biding its time.

I guess it comes down to I have so much more I want to experience and do and be and write about in this sliver of light between infinities. I may get tired, I may even feel like I don't want to get back up . . .

But it's in service of others—my boys, my Beth, my friends, my Davids, my community—that I find my footing and pedal on.